MW00562735

Study Guide for the
ParaPro Assessment

► ► ► ► ► ► ► ► ► ► ►

A PUBLICATION OF EDUCATIONAL TESTING SERVICE

Copyright © 2003 by Educational Testing Service.
EDUCATIONAL TESTING SERVICE, ETS, the ETS logo, and THE PRAXIS SERIES: PROFESSIONAL ASSESSMENTS FOR BEGINNING
TEACHERS and its logo are registered trademarks of Educational Testing Service. SAT is a registered trademark of the College Entrance Examination
Board. THE PRAXIS SERIES is a trademark of Educational Testing Service.

Table of Contents

Study Guide for the *ParaPro Assessment*

▶   ▶   ▶   ▶   ▶   ▶   ▶   ▶   ▶   ▶   ▶   ▶

TABLE OF CONTENTS

Chapter 1

Introduction to the *ParaPro Assessment* and Suggestions for Using this Study Guide

▶   ▶   ▶   ▶   ▶   ▶   ▶   ▶   ▶   ▶   ▶   ▶

Background on the *ParaPro Assessment*

The *ParaPro Assessment* is designed for prospective and practicing paraprofessionals in education. The test measures skills and knowledge in reading, mathematics, and writing, as well as the ability to apply those skills and knowledge to assist in classroom instruction.

The *ParaPro Assessment* was developed in response to the federal legislation known as *No Child Left Behind*, which was signed into law by President Bush in January 2002. The law mandates that beginning January 8, 2002, paraprofessionals be required to have one of the following:

- An associate of arts degree

- Two years of college

- A passing score on a test that measures reading, writing, and mathematics and the ability to assist in the instruction of reading, writing, and mathematics

The choice of test or tests to satisfy the third option is left to the discretion of states and districts.

About the *ParaPro Assessment*

The *ParaPro Assessment* reflects the most current research and the professional judgment and experience of educators across the country. The test was developed with the assistance of paraprofessionals and teachers who work with paraprofessionals.

The *ParaPro Assessment* consists of 90 multiple-choice questions and covers six major areas, in the following proportions:

Content Category	Approximate Number of Questions	Approximate Percentage of Examination
Reading Skills and Knowledge	18	20%
Application of Reading Skills and Knowledge to Classroom Instruction	12	13%
Mathematics Skills and Knowledge	18	20%
Application of Mathematics Skills and Knowledge to Classroom Instruction	12	13%
Writing Skills and Knowledge	18	20%
Application of Writing Skills and Knowledge to Classroom Instruction	12	13%

For each of the three subject areas—reading, mathematics, and writing—approximately two-thirds of the questions focus on basic skills and knowledge, and approximately one-third of the questions focus on how those skills and knowledge apply to classroom instruction. Fifteen of the questions in the test (five in each subject) are pretest questions and do not count toward your score. The test questions are arranged by subject area, with reading first, then mathematics, and then writing.

The *ParaPro Assessment* may be taken either in paper-and-pencil form or on computer. Both versions have the same questions and allow you the same amount of time to complete the test: $2\frac{1}{2}$ hours. Use of a calculator is not allowed.

The three sections of the test are not timed separately, so you should decide how much time you can spend on each section. If you want to budget your time equally across all three sections, you probably should not spend more than 50 minutes on each section. However, you may find when you take the practice test included in chapter 7 of this guide that some sections go faster than others. Based on your experience with the practice test, you can adjust the time that you allow yourself for each section of the actual test.

How to Use this Book

This book gives you instruction, practice, and test-taking tips to help you prepare for taking the *ParaPro Assessment*. In chapters 1, 2, and 3, you will find an overview of the test, information about signing up for the test and taking it on computer, and general test-taking suggestions. Chapters 4, 5, and 6 provide review courses in reading, math, and writing so you can refresh your understanding of the important principles you'll need to know for the test. These chapters also contain sample questions to help you become familiar with the question formats that will actually appear on the test and to help you understand the kinds of knowledge and reasoning you will need to apply to choose correct answers. Chapter 7 contains a complete practice test, and chapter 8 contains the answers to the questions in the practice test, along with explanations of those answers.

So where should you start? Well, all users of this book will probably want to begin with the following two steps:

Become familiar with the test content. Note what chapters 4, 5, and 6 say about the topics covered in the test. For easy reference, appendix C includes a list of the topics covered in all three subjects—reading, math, and writing—in one place.

Consider how well you know the content in each subject area. Perhaps you already know that you need to build up your skills in a particular area—reading, math, or writing. If you're not sure, skim over chapters 4, 5, and 6 to see what topics they cover. If you encounter material that feels unfamiliar or difficult, fold down page corners or insert sticky notes to remind yourself to spend extra time in these sections.

Also, all users of this book will probably want to end with these two steps:

Familiarize yourself with test taking. Chapter 3 is designed to answer frequently asked questions about the *ParaPro Assessment*, such as whether it is a good idea to guess on the test. You can simulate the experience of the test by taking the practice test in chapter 7. Choose a time and place where you will not be interrupted or distracted. Then, using chapter 8, score your responses. The scoring key identifies which topic each question addresses, so you can see which areas are your strongest and weakest. Look over the explanations of the questions you missed, and see whether you understand them and could answer similar questions correctly. Then plan any additional studying according to what you've learned about your understanding of the topics.

Register for the test and consider last-minute tips. Consult chapter 2 about how to register for the test, and review the checklist in chapter 9 to make sure you are ready for the test.

What you do between these first steps and these last steps depends on whether you intend to use this book to prepare on your own or as part of a class or study group.

Using this book to prepare on your own:

If you are working by yourself to prepare for the *ParaPro Assessment*, you may find it helpful to use the following approach:

Fill out the Study Plan Sheet in appendix A. This worksheet will help you to focus on what topics you need to study most, identify materials that will help you study, and set a schedule for doing the studying. The last item is particularly important if you know you tend to put off work.

Use other materials to reinforce chapters 4, 5, and 6. These chapters contain review courses in reading, math, and writing, but you may want to get additional help for the topics that give you the most trouble. For example, if you know you have a problem with spelling, you can find lists of frequently misspelled words in books and on the Internet. Math textbooks can provide instruction and give you additional practice with math problems. Computer-based instruction with a system such as the PLATO® ParaPro Preparation Package may also help you improve your skills in reading, math, and writing. See appendix B for more information about the PLATO® ParaPro Preparation Package.

Using this book as part of a study group:

People who have a lot of studying to do sometimes find it helpful to form a study group with others who are preparing toward the same goal. Study groups give members opportunities to ask questions and get detailed answers. In a group, some members usually have a better understanding of certain topics, while others in the group are better at other topics. As members take turns explaining concepts to each other, everyone builds self-confidence. If the group encounters a question that none of the members can answer well, the members can go as a group to a teacher or other expert and get answers efficiently. Because study groups schedule regular meetings, group members study in a more disciplined fashion. They also gain emotional support. The group should be large enough so that various people can contribute various kinds of knowledge, but small enough so that it stays focused. Often three to six people is a good size.

Here are some ways to use this book as part of a study group:

Plan the group's study program. Parts of the Study Plan Sheet in appendix A can help to structure your group's study program. By filling out the first five columns and sharing the work sheets, everyone will learn more about your group's mix of abilities and about the resources (such as textbooks) that members can share with the group. In the sixth column ("Dates planned for study of content"), you can create an overall schedule for your group's study program.

Plan individual group sessions. At the end of each session, the group should decide what specific topics will be covered at the next meeting and who will be the presenter of each topic. Use the topic headings and subheadings in chapters 4, 5, and 6 to select topics. Some sessions might be based on topics from the review courses contained in these chapters; other sessions might be based on the sample questions from these chapters.

Prepare your presentation for the group. When it's your turn to be presenter, prepare something that's more than a lecture. If you are presenting material from the review course part of a chapter, write five to ten original questions to pose to the group. Practicing writing actual questions can help you better understand the topics covered on the test as well as the types of questions you will encounter on the test. It will also give other members of the group extra practice at answering questions. If you are presenting material from the sample questions, use each sample question as a model for writing at least one original question.

Take the practice test together. The idea of chapter 7 is to simulate an actual administration of the test, so scheduling a test session with the group will add to the realism and will also help boost everyone's confidence.

Learn from the results of the practice test. Use chapter 8 to score each other's answer sheets. Then plan one or more study sessions based on the questions that group members got wrong. For example, each group member might be responsible for a question that he or she got wrong and could use it as a model to create an original question to pose to the group, together with an explanation of the correct answer modeled after the explanations in chapter 8.

Whether you decide to study alone or with a group, remember that the best way to prepare is to have an organized plan. The plan should set goals based on specific topics and skills that you need to learn, and it should commit you to a realistic set of deadlines for meeting these goals. Then you need to discipline yourself to stick with your plan and accomplish your goals on schedule.

In the next chapter, you will find information about practical matters, including how to register for the test and tips for taking the computer-based version of the test.

Chapter 2

Practical Matters: Signing Up for the Test and
Tips for the Computer Version

▶   ▶   ▶   ▶   ▶   ▶   ▶   ▶   ▶   ▶   ▶   ▶

Signing up for the Test and Getting Your Scores

If you want to take the paper-and-pencil version of the *ParaPro Assessment*, use the form and preaddressed envelope in the *Praxis ParaPro Registration Bulletin*. You may order the registration bulletin from the ETS ParaPro Web site at http://www.ets.org/parapro.

You may also call or write Educational Testing Service:

The Praxis Series
Educational Testing Service
P.O. Box 6051
Princeton, NJ 08541-6051
Phone: 609-771-7395
Disability Services: 609-771-7780
TTY only: 609-771-7714

If you take the paper-and-pencil version of the test, your official score report will arrive in the mail approximately four weeks after your test date. Your score report will contain your overall score and six area scores.

If you are taking the computer version of the *ParaPro Assessment*, you do not have to preregister with Educational Testing Service. To take the computer version, contact the appropriate person in your school or district to find out how you can arrange a day and time for taking the test. Once you are seated at the computer and the school or district administrator has entered the correct codes to start the test, you will be asked to fill in your name, address, and other information on the registration screen. At the end of the testing session, you will receive an unofficial report of your score. Two weeks later, you will receive an official score report in the mail that will contain your overall score and six area scores.

Taking the Test on Computer

The computer-based version of the *ParaPro Assessment* has the same questions as the paper-and-pencil version and takes the same amount of time. You need only a beginner's level of computer skill to take the computer-based version of the *ParaPro Assessment*. The test runs in an Internet browser. If you have spent an hour surfing the Internet, you know enough about how to work the mouse and how to click on buttons. If you do not have experience with computers, the mouse, and the Internet, visit your public library and ask someone to help you get started. Surf around until you feel comfortable making choices with the mouse.

What the computer-based version looks like

Most of the screens you will see when you take the computer-based version of the *ParaPro Assessment* will look like this:

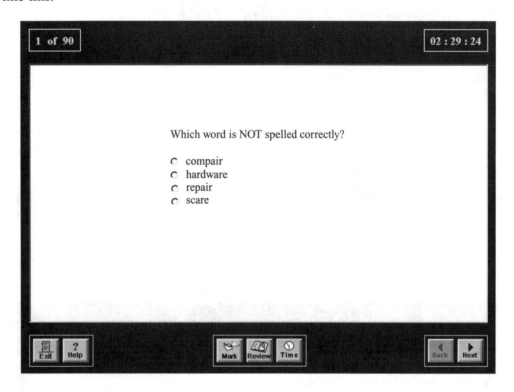

Note how the screen is laid out:

- In the upper left-hand corner you can see which question you are now working on (question 1 of 90).

- In the upper right-hand corner you can see how much time you have left. You can hide or display the clock by clicking [Time]. (During the last 10 minutes of the test, the clock remains on continuously.)

- The test questions appear in the middle of the screen. You simply click the radio button next to your answer choice. You can change your answer by clicking on another radio button.

- When you're ready to move to the next question, click [Next].

- To return to the previous question, click [Back].

- To mark a question so you can review it later, click 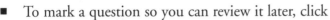 .

- To check your progress or review a question, click . The Review screen lists all questions, and for each one indicates whether you have seen it, answered it, and/or marked it. From this screen you can select any question and jump to it. You can also see at a glance whether you have skipped any questions. (There is no penalty for guessing on the *ParaPro Assessment*, so you should try to answer every question.)

- Help is always available. Just click to see instructions about the *ParaPro Assessment*.

- To exit the test, click . Before you exit the test, it is a good idea to click the Review button to make sure you have answered every question.

In the reading and writing sections, when you are given a long passage of text accompanied by several questions, the screen is divided and looks like this:

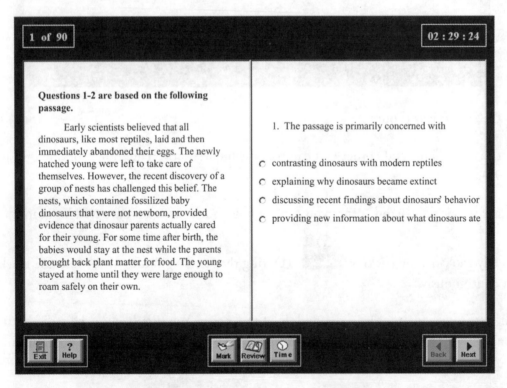

Note that in the heading for the passage (above on the left), it says that two questions are based on the passage. After you answer the first question and click the "Next" button, the right side of the screen changes to show you the next question about the passage.

After you complete the test and exit, you will be able to print your unofficial score report using your Internet browser's Print button. You will receive seven scores: six sub-scores and an overall scaled score.

You can access an on-line tutorial for the *ParaPro Assessment*. Go to http://www.ets.org/parapro. The tutorial shows examples of the screens, explains how to use the buttons, and familiarizes you with the screens and procedures for taking the test on computer. No matter what your level of experience with computers, you probably will want to look at the on-line tutorial before you take the test. If you know what to expect, you will feel less anxious on the day you take the test. (You will also be able to access the on-line tutorial immediately before you take your test.)

In the next chapter, you will find some additional suggestions for minimizing anxiety about taking tests.

Chapter 3

Do Tests Make You Nervous? Try These Tips

► ► ► ► ► ► ► ► ► ► ► ►

It's natural to be nervous for a test such as the *ParaPro Assessment*. You can use your nervous energy to strengthen your performance on the test if you approach it with these facts in mind:

- There are no trick questions on the test. (Some questions may be difficult for you, but they were not written in order to trick you or other test takers.)

- You should have plenty of time to complete the test. Two and a half (2½) hours is a long time for answering 90 questions, so you should not have to feel rushed.

- The test questions are worded very carefully by the test writers and are reviewed many times to make sure that the questions are clear about what they are asking. If a question seems confusing at first, take some time to reread it more slowly.

- You have choices during the test: you can skip a question and come back to it later; you can change your answer to any question at any time during the testing session; you can mark questions you want to return to later.

The sections below give you facts about the test and suggestions for maximizing your performance.

General Test-Taking Suggestions

The *ParaPro Assessment* contains a mixture of types of questions. Some of these are simple identification questions, such as "What is the name of the shape shown above?" But other types of questions require you to analyze situations, synthesize material, and apply knowledge to specific examples. In short, they require you to think and solve problems. This type of question is usually longer than a simple identification question and takes more time to answer. You may be presented with something to read (a description of a classroom situation, a sample of student work, a chart or graph) and then asked to answer questions based on your reading. Good reading skills are required, and you must read carefully. Both on this test and as a paraprofessional, you will need to process and use what you read efficiently.

If you know that your reading skills are not strong, you may want to take a reading course. Community colleges and night schools often have reading labs that can help you strengthen your reading skills.

Useful facts about the test

1. You can answer the questions in any order. You can go through the questions from beginning to end, as many test takers do, or you can create your own path. Perhaps you will want to answer questions in your strongest subject first and then move from your strengths to your weaker areas. There is no right or wrong way. Use the approach that works for you.

2. Don't worry about answer patterns. There is one myth that says that answers on multiple-choice tests follow patterns. There is another myth that there will never be more than two questions with the same lettered answer following each other. There is no truth to either of these myths. Select the answer you think is correct, based on your knowledge of the subject.

3. There is no penalty for guessing. Your test score is based on the number of correct answers you have, and incorrect answers are not counted against you. When you don't know the answer to a question, try to eliminate any obviously wrong answers and then guess at the correct one.

4. It's OK to write in your test booklet. If you are taking the paper-and-pencil version of the test, you can work problems right on the pages of the booklet, make notes to yourself, or mark questions you want to review later. Your test booklet will be destroyed after you are finished with it, so use it in any way that is helpful to you. If you are taking the test on computer, you can work problems on scratch paper and mark questions using the "Mark" button.

Smart tips for taking the test

1. Put your answers in the right "bubbles." It seems obvious, but if you are taking the paper-and-pencil version, you should make sure you are "bubbling in" the answer to the right question on your answer sheet. Check the question number each time you fill in an answer. Use a Number 2 lead pencil and be sure that each mark is heavy and dark and completely fills the answer space. If you change an answer, be sure the previous mark is erased completely. For the computer-based version, be sure that the circle next to your chosen answer is dark after you have clicked on it.

2. Be prepared for questions that use the words *LEAST, EXCEPT,* or *NOT*. Some questions may ask you to select the choice that doesn't fit or that contains information that is not true. Questions in this format use the words *LEAST, EXCEPT,* or *NOT*. The words are capitalized when they appear in test questions to signal a difference in what you are being asked to look for: you are looking for the single answer choice that is different in some specified way from the other answer choices. Here is an example of a question in this format that might be on the writing part of the test:

Which word is NOT spelled correctly?

(A) compair
(B) hardware
(C) repair
(D) scare

In the question above, three of the four words are spelled correctly, and one is NOT. The word that is NOT spelled correctly is the correct answer choice—in this case, (A). The word in (A) should be spelled "compare."

When you encounter a *NOT, LEAST,* or *EXCEPT* question, it is a good idea to reread the question after you select your answer to make sure that you have answered the question correctly.

3. Skip the questions you find to be extremely difficult. There are bound to be some questions that you think are hard. Rather than trying to answer these on your first pass through the test, leave them blank and mark them in your test booklet so that you can come back to them. (If you are taking the test on computer, you can click the "Mark" button to mark a question and then use the "Review" page to see which questions you have marked.) Pay attention to the time as you answer the rest of the questions on the test and try to finish with 10 or 15 minutes remaining so that you can go back over the questions you left blank. Even if you don't know the answers the second time you read the questions, see whether you can narrow down the possible answers, and then guess.

4. Keep track of the time. For the paper-and-pencil version, bring a watch to the test, just in case the clock in the test room is difficult for you to see. (For the computer version, there is a clock on the screen.) Remember that, on average, you have a little more than $1\frac{1}{2}$ minutes to answer each of the questions. One and a half ($1\frac{1}{2}$) minutes may not seem like much time, but you will be able to answer a number of questions in only a few seconds each. You will probably have plenty of time to answer all of the questions, but if you find yourself becoming bogged down in one section, you might decide to move on and come back to that section later.

5. Read all of the possible answers before selecting one—and then reread the question to be sure the answer you have selected really answers the question being asked.

6. Check your answers. If you have extra time left over at the end of the test, look over each question and make sure that you have filled in the "bubble" on the answer sheet (or on the computer screen) as you intended. Many test takers make careless mistakes that could have been corrected if they had checked their answers.

7. Don't worry about your score when you are taking the test. No one is expected to get all of the questions correct. Your score on this test is not analogous to your score on the SAT or other similar tests. It doesn't matter on this test whether you score very high or barely pass. If you meet the minimum passing scores for your state or district, you will have fulfilled the requirement.

The Day of the Test

You should complete your review process a day or two before the actual test date. And many clichés you may have heard about the day of the test are true. You should

- Be well rested

- Take photo identification with you

- Take a supply of well-sharpened No. 2 pencils (at least three) if you are taking the paper-and-pencil version

- Eat before you take the test, and take some food or a snack to keep your energy level up

- Be prepared to stand in line to check in or to wait while other test takers are being checked in

You can't control the testing situation, but you can control yourself. Stay calm. The supervisors are well trained and make every effort to provide uniform testing conditions, but don't let it bother you if the test doesn't start exactly on time. You will have the necessary amount of time once it does start.

You can think of preparing for this test as training for an athletic event. Once you've trained, and prepared, and rested, give it everything you've got. Good luck.

Chapter 4

Reading Review Course with Sample Questions

▶ ▶ ▶ ▶ ▶ ▶ ▶ ▶ ▶ ▶ ▶ ▶

Overview

The 30 questions in the reading section of the *ParaPro Assessment* fall into two categories:

I. Reading Skills and Knowledge (approximately 18 questions)

II. Application of Reading Skills and Knowledge to Classroom Instruction (approximately 12 questions)

All questions are multiple-choice. The first category of questions tests your ability to understand, interpret, and analyze a wide range of text. These questions may look familiar to you, since they are similar to reading comprehension questions you may have encountered on other multiple-choice tests. To answer each question, you are asked to read a brief passage or examine a graphic text (such as a table, diagram, chart, or graph).

The second category of questions tests your ability to *apply* your reading skills and knowledge to classroom instruction. These questions look slightly different from questions you may have seen on other tests because they present an actual classroom situation or activity, but to answer them you need only apply your reading knowledge and skills. You do *not* need special knowledge of reading pedagogy (philosophies or approaches to teaching reading).

Part I: The Reading Skills and Knowledge Section

The Reading Skills and Knowledge questions are based on reading passages, as well as tables, diagrams, charts, and graphs. Some passages and graphic texts are the basis for only one question; others are the basis for more than one question. The reading passages vary in difficulty and in length.

The subject matter of the passages also varies. The passages cover a variety of subjects in the areas of social science, humanities, science, and general interest. Be prepared to encounter many different styles of writing. For example, a passage that objectively describes a scientific discovery may be followed by a personal memoir.

You may know a lot about some of the topics and next to nothing about others. That does not matter: *to answer the questions, you do not need to draw on any background or outside knowledge.* Everything you need to know to answer the questions is directly stated or implied in the passages.

In some cases, the information in the passage may conflict with knowledge you have about the subject. If it does, you should not let your knowledge influence your choice of answer: *always answer each question on the basis of what is stated or implied in the given passage.*

What's Being Tested?

Below is a list of the types of Reading Skills and Knowledge questions you may encounter. Each of these types will be explained in greater detail on the following pages.

You may be asked to

- identify the main idea or primary purpose of a passage

- identify supporting ideas

- identify how a reading selection is organized

- determine the meanings of words or phrases in context

- draw inferences or implications from directly stated content

- determine whether information is presented as fact or opinion

- interpret information from tables, diagrams, charts, and graphs

You do not need to identify which type of question is being asked in order to answer the question. However, your awareness of the different types of questions will help you move through the material quickly and find the information you need from the passages more easily.

General Test-Taking Tips for Reading-Skills Questions

- **Read the passage.** It may sound obvious to mention reading the passage as a tip, but there are a lot of test preparation guides for reading tests that recommend only skimming a reading passage. Skimming is a useful strategy for locating specific pieces of information, but it cannot substitute for careful reading of a passage. You are much more likely to do well on the reading questions if you have read the passage carefully and have a clear sense of it as a whole. You should have plenty of time to read each passage carefully and still be able to finish the rest of the test.

- **Don't spend too much time worrying about what you don't understand.** Even though you should read carefully, be prepared for the fact that there may be some vocabulary or information in the passage that is unfamiliar to you. Don't spend too much time trying to figure out very difficult parts of a passage. You may not need to understand everything in the passage to answer the questions for the passage correctly.

- **Work methodically.** After you read the passage, answer each question. Refer back to the passage as necessary to confirm your answer choice. For some questions, it may now be appropriate to skim the passage for the information needed to answer the question.

- **Answer all of the questions for each passage.** Work through all of the questions for each passage before moving on to the next passage. For other parts of the *ParaPro Assessment* it might make sense to leave some questions unanswered and come back to them. For the Reading Skills section, however, you should try to answer all of the questions that refer to a passage at one time. This technique helps you move quickly through the test because you will not have to spend time rereading passages.

- **Read all of the answer choices.** Always read all of the answer choices before you select your answer. You are to choose the best answer, so you must read all of the choices to determine which is best.

- **Consider only what the question asks.** Be sure to find the answer choice that answers only what the question asks. Often there are other choices that contain information that appears in the passage but that is not directly relevant to the question. After you select the choice you believe to be the answer, reread the question to make sure it directly answers the question.

REVIEW COURSE: Reading Skills and Knowledge

Making sense of the passages

Strong readers use a number of techniques to help them better understand a passage. One technique is to identify three essential elements of the passage: its *main idea*, its *organization*, and *keywords and concepts* that appear in the passage. If you have a general sense of these three elements before you answer the questions, you will know where to look in the passage to confirm your answer.

1. **Locate the main idea.** What central idea connects all of the information in a passage together? This is the main idea of the passage.

2. **Look at the organization.** How are different parts of the passage related to each other? For example, does the writer ask a question and answer it? Describe an idea and give an example? In a short passage, look at the role played by each sentence. In a longer passage, look at the role played by each paragraph. (Some passages do not have a very clear or apparent organizational structure, so do not spend a lot of time searching for the structure if you cannot see it; you may not need to know this to answer the questions.)

3. **Identify keywords and concepts.** As you read the passage, take note of any important *keywords and concepts*. Look for frequently repeated words or phrases. Identifying these words and phrases will help you concentrate on the important ideas in the passage.

Once you have a basic understanding of the main idea, organization, and keywords and concepts in the passage, you are ready to tackle the questions that accompany it. Below are detailed descriptions of each of the 7 question types in the *ParaPro Assessment*, along with sample questions and explanations.

1 Understanding the main idea or primary purpose

Main idea questions ask about the central point of a passage. The main idea ties all of the sentences in a passage together; each of the sentences expresses, supports, or develops the main idea. A main idea is sometimes directly stated, and sometimes it is the first sentence in a passage. However, a main idea may appear at any point in a piece of writing, and may, in fact, not be explicitly stated at all.

Here is the way in which main idea questions are usually asked:

■   The main idea of the passage is . . .

Primary purpose questions ask about the purpose of the passage or the author's purpose in writing the passage. Some common primary purposes involve defining, describing, refuting, or explaining. Sometimes the language of a passage may offer clues as to the purpose of the passage. For example, an author may use words associated with predicting, such as "probably" or "in the future"; words associated with persuading, such as "should" or "ought"; or emotional language that indicates a personal purpose.

Here are the ways in which primary purpose questions are usually asked:

■   The passage is primarily concerned with . . .

■   The primary purpose of the passage is to . . .

■   The author's purpose in writing this passage is most likely to . . .

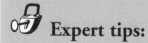 **Expert tips:**

- Keep in mind that the question asks about the *main* idea and the *primary* purpose. You must distinguish between minor details and main ideas in the passage. Minor ideas are usually mentioned only once or twice. Main ideas are mentioned several times and often explored in several different ways.

- Look for the choice that is a description of the main idea or primary purpose of the *entire* passage.

- One way to identify the purpose of a passage is to ask, "What did the author *do* in this passage?" Use words like *demonstrate*, *show*, *question*, or *persuade* to answer the question. This technique focuses you on the author's goals for the passage.

- Don't confuse the *topic* of a passage with its main idea or purpose. All of the choices may refer to the topic of the passage (e.g., elephants), but only one choice represents the main idea (e.g., "Scientists have found evidence that elephants experience emotions").

- Don't choose something with which you think the author would agree, but which is not discussed or hinted at in the passage. That idea may not be the main point the author was making in the passage.

- Don't just look for the choices that have wording that is most similar to that used in the passage. Often, *all* choices borrow wording from the passage. You will need to read both the passage and the choices carefully to find the correct answer.

- Be sure that the choice you select doesn't go *beyond* the passage—sometimes a choice may present information that is not actually in the given passage.

 **Let's Try It!**

Now let's work through a sample question using the skills and strategies you have learned on the previous pages.

The following passage is excerpted from Maya Angelou's memoir *I Know Why the Caged Bird Sings*.

Until I was thirteen and left Arkansas for good, the Store was my favorite place to be. Alone and empty in the mornings, it looked like an unopened present from a stranger. Opening the front doors was pulling the ribbon off the unexpected gift. The light would come in softly (we faced north), easing itself over the shelves of mackerel, salmon, tobacco, thread.

---

1. In the passage, Angelou is primarily concerned with

    (A) outlining her chores in the Store
    (B) describing the items most often sold in the Store
    (C) discussing her perception of the Store
    (D) explaining why she left Arkansas

Answer

You can recognize this as a "primary purpose" question by the language of the question; it asks you to identify what the passage is *primarily concerned with*. The topic of the passage is the Store; all of the sentences in the passage refer explicitly or implicitly to the Store. The passage describes what the Store *looks* like to the author; thus choice (C), "discussing her *perception* of the Store," is the best answer. While choice (A) refers to the Store, it mentions information that does not appear in the passage. Choice (B) refers to the Store, but although the passage identifies some items sold in the store, it does not identify the items most often sold there. Choice (D) refers to a detail in the passage, but it does not reflect the author's primary purpose for the entire passage.

2 Understanding supporting ideas

Supporting ideas are ideas used to support or elaborate on the main idea. Often supporting ideas offer facts, details, and definitions that refer to the main topic. Whereas questions about the main idea ask you to determine the meaning of a passage or a paragraph as a whole, questions about supporting ideas ask you to determine the meaning of a particular part of the passage.

Supporting ideas provide additional information but do not change the main idea or primary purpose of the passage. For example, in the passage by Maya Angelou above, the information presented in the last sentence ("the light would come in softly, easing itself over the shelves") explains an important aspect of the Store's appearance, but does not change the primary purpose of the passage—to discuss the author's perception of the Store. Therefore, the detail about the light *supports* that primary purpose by offering a specific example of the author's perception of the Store.

Supporting idea questions often ask you to distinguish between closely related but distinct details, identify causes or effects, locate examples, or find specific content.

Here are the ways in which supporting idea questions are usually asked:

- According to the passage, X is . . .

- The author's description of X mentions . . .

- The passage states that one of the consequences of X was . . .

- According to the passage, X is immediately followed by . . .

- The passage mentions all of the following EXCEPT . . .

🔦 Expert tips:

- Eliminate the choices that present information not given in the passage.

- Eliminate the choices that present information contradictory to what is presented in the passage.

You'll get a chance to try out this type of question soon, but first consider another type of question.

3 Understanding vocabulary in context

Some questions ask you to identify the meanings of words as they are used in the context of a passage. These questions do NOT test your prior knowledge of difficult or unusual words. Instead, they test your ability to understand how a word is being used in the context of a particular passage. All of the information you need to answer the question is provided in the passage. In fact, most of the words you will encounter in vocabulary in context questions are probably already very familiar to you.

The *context* of a passage is the specific situation described in the passage. Sometimes words and phrases can change meaning depending on the situation in which they are used. For example, the word "cool" could be used to refer to temperature: "It was a cool October day." It could also be used as a synonym for "calm": "In the chaos caused by the accident, Maria remained cool and collected." In order to determine which meaning is appropriate, you need to look at the other words in the passage to establish the situation being described.

Sometimes writers use unusual words or figures of speech (words not intended to be understood literally) in order to express their ideas. For example, in the sentence "After Sean won the spelling bee he was walking on air," the phrase "walking on air" is a figure of speech. It is not meant to be taken literally; instead, it is meant to convey Sean's exhilaration at winning the spelling bee. When you are asked about an unusual word or figure of speech, you are given sufficient context to help you identify the word.

If you don't know the word, you can still answer the question. You should be able to figure out its meaning from the surrounding parts of the passage.

Here are the ways in which vocabulary in context questions are usually asked:

- In the context of the passage, the word X most nearly means . . .

- The author most probably uses the word X in line *y* to mean . . .

- The author uses the phrase "XYZ" to indicate that . . .

Expert tips:

- Remember that the question is not simply asking about the meaning of a specific word; it is asking about its meaning *in the context of the passage*. Therefore, do not simply choose an option that provides a correct meaning; often all the choices offer acceptable meanings of the word. Your job is to choose which meaning makes the most sense as the word is used in the passage.

- Reread the relevant sentence in the passage, using the word or phrase you have chosen from the answer choices. Confirm that the new sentence makes sense in the context of the passage as a whole.

Let's Try It!

Now let's work through some samples of "supporting idea" and "vocabulary in context" questions.

Questions 2–4 are based on the following passage.

Line

5

> Throughout the world, there are places where the wind piles sand into strange hills and ridges called dunes. Interestingly, some sand dunes can be heard as well as seen. Dunes may squeak, roar, sing, or boom when disturbed. The sound a particular sand dune makes is determined by the way sand is distributed.
>
> Scientists who have studied the sand grains from dunes under special microscopes found that the grains must be highly polished, perfectly smooth round balls in order to produce sounds. The grains must be absolutely dry and are usually especially small. Dunes that make noise are usually composed mostly of quartz sand.

---

2. The type of sound made by a sand dune is determined by the

   (A) temperature of the air
   (B) way the sand is arranged
   (C) amount of wind around the dune
   (D) weight of the sand

Answer

This question asks you to identify a specific detail—what determines the type of sound made by the sand dune. Look at the idea indicated in the question and locate the discussion of that idea in the passage. This occurs at the end of the first paragraph: "The sound a particular sand dune makes is determined by the way sand is distributed." Then look for synonyms of the description in the answers: "arranged" is a synonym for "distributed." This confirms that the correct answer is (B).

3. In order to produce sounds, sand grains must be all of the following EXCEPT

   (A) round
   (B) polished
   (C) large
   (D) dry

Answer

Note the format of this question. When you see the word "EXCEPT" in a question, you are being asked to identify the one option that is NOT presented in the passage. Choices (A), (B), and (D) can be eliminated because these details are specifically mentioned in the text. Choice (C), however, is not mentioned; in fact, the passage claims that the sand grains are usually especially *small* to produce sounds (line 7). Thus (C) is the correct choice.

4. In the context of the passage, "smooth" (line 6) most nearly means

 (A) even
 (B) easy
 (C) bland
 (D) agreeable

Answer

This question asks you to determine the meaning of the word in context. "Smooth" is not a difficult word, but it does have several meanings, so you must look at the context in which the word is used to answer the question correctly. First, locate the sentence in which the word "smooth" is used. The sentence in lines 5–7 describes the grains of sand as "highly polished, perfectly smooth round balls." Then substitute each of the words listed as the answer choices for the word "smooth"; the only word that makes sense in the context of the sentence is (A), "even."

4 Understanding the organization of a passage

Organization refers to how the information presented in a reading passage is arranged to achieve the author's purpose. The organization of a passage reflects the relationship between the individual sentences and the ideas in the passage.

Sometimes a question asks you to identify how a passage as a whole is constructed. For example, a passage might introduce and describe a theory, compare and then contrast two points of view, or offer an idea and then refute it.

Sometimes a question asks you to identify how one paragraph or sentence is related to another. For instance, the second paragraph of a passage may provide examples of a phenomenon described in the first paragraph, or the second paragraph could refute a theory presented in the first paragraph. The answers to these questions may be expressed in general terms (e.g., "a hypothesis is explained and then challenged") or in terms specific to the passage (e.g., "The architectural style of buildings in the nineteenth-century United States is described and then a specific building is discussed in more detail").

As another way of testing your ability to recognize organization, you may be asked to identify why an author includes a specific piece of information. Examples of such purposes for including information might be to support an assertion, to provide an example, or to contradict a claim.

To answer organization questions, pay attention to how sentences and paragraphs are connected. Sometimes signal words like "for example," "however," or "another reason" can make such connections explicit by telling you whether a sentence or paragraph is giving an example, offering a contrast, or providing additional information. You may want to take note of these kinds of words as you read through the passage for the first time. However, such signal words might not always appear in the passage. When you cannot find signal words, you must ask yourself how one sentence or paragraph is connected to another.

Here are the ways in which organization questions are usually asked:

- How is the information presented in the passage organized?

- The author mentions X most likely in order to . . .

- Which statement best describes the organization of the passage?

 Expert tips:

- The following words are often used in the answer choices of organization questions, so it will be helpful for you to know the meanings of these terms: *define, compare, refute, summarize, criticize, analogy, generalization, theory, hypothesis, phenomenon, cause-and-effect,* and *chronological.*

- If you are asked to identify why the author includes a particular detail, consider the overall purpose of the passage. The author includes a particular detail because the detail contributes to the author's overall purpose.

- Similarly, the overall organization of a passage is often parallel to its purpose. For instance, a passage whose purpose is to offer a theory and then refute it may be organized into two paragraphs, one that describes the theory and another that explains why the theory doesn't work.

Let's Try It!

Many pet owners find that their pets are waiting at the door when the owners arrive home. Researchers have offered a number of theories to account for the pets' behavior. One is that the pets may be responding to events coinciding with their owners' arrival (their owners may always arrive at home shortly after the mail is delivered). Another possibility is that the pets are responding to sensory cues that elude us (the pet may recognize the unique sound of the owner's car when the car is some distance away).

---

5. Which statement best describes the organization of the passage as a whole?

   (A) A phenomenon is described and then two examples of it are provided.
   (B) A phenomenon is described and then two possible explanations for it are presented.
   (C) A theory is proposed and then shown to be incorrect.
   (D) A problem is presented and then two solutions for it are provided.

Answer

Approach this question by looking at each sentence in the passage. The passage begins by presenting a phenomenon—that pets are waiting at the door for their owners when the owners come home (sentence 1). Then the passage indicates that researchers have offered a number of theories to explain this behavior (sentence 2). The passage goes on to provide two possible explanations for why pets may be waiting for their owners when they come home (sentences 3 and 4). Thus answer (B), describing a phenomenon and offering two explanations for it, is correct.

5 Drawing inferences or implications from directly stated content

An inference is a statement that is clearly suggested or implied by the author; an inference is *based on* information given in the passage, but the statement itself is not given in the passage. To answer inference questions, you may have to draw conclusions from the information presented. For example, if a passage explicitly states an effect, a question could ask you to infer its cause. Be ready, therefore, to concentrate not only on the explicit meanings of the author's words, but also on what those words imply.

We use inferences in conversations all of the time. Here is an example:

Tina: "Did you buy a blue sports car?"

Carrie: "The manufacturer offers that model of car only in black, red, and silver."

Tina should be able to *infer* that Carrie did not buy a blue car, even though Carrie did not explicitly say so. Because no blue cars were made, it would not be possible for Carrie to buy a blue one.

Inference questions often ask you to apply a general statement to a specific situation. In the example above, the general statement that only red, black, and silver cars are offered has implications for Carrie's specific purchase; she could not buy a blue car.

Here are the ways in which inference questions are usually asked:

- The passage suggests that X would happen when . . .

- The author of the passage implies that X . . .

- It can be inferred from the passage that X is effective in all of the following ways EXCEPT . . .

Expert tips:

- Go back to the passage and find the information that may relate to the question.

- Formulate in your own words the answer to the question, and then find the choice that most closely matches your answer.

- Make sure your answer does not contradict the main idea of the passage.

- Make sure your answer does not go too far and make assumptions that are not indicated in the passage. (For example, in the conversation between Carrie and Tina, Tina would have gone too far if she had said, "So a sports car could never be blue." This cannot be inferred from Carrie's statement because she makes the statement about only one manufacturer; she is not making a statement about all car manufacturers.)

- You should be able to defend your selection by pointing to explicitly stated information in the passage that leads to the inference you have selected.

Let's Try It!

The novelist Zane Grey was one of the early writers of the type of novel called the western. Today, however, modern historians dismiss Grey's romanticized description of the early American West. They point out that the Old West was actually a place of pointless violence and willful destruction of natural resources. And yet, Grey's fiction about the Old West continues to exert a powerful hold on the American imagination.

---

6. The passage suggests that modern historians find that Grey's books

   (A) focus too much on the pointless violence of the Old West
   (B) inaccurately portray life in the Old West
   (C) contain imaginative descriptions of the Old West that readers enjoy today
   (D) realistically portray the loss of natural resources in the Old West

Answer

The passage explains the attitudes of modern historians towards Grey's description of the Old West. The historians "dismiss Grey's romanticized description of the early American West," which suggests that Grey's descriptions are not credible. Thus answer (B), which describes Grey's books as being inaccurate, is the best choice.

6 Distinguishing between fact and opinion

Often a piece of writing contains both facts and opinions, and you are asked to distinguish one from the other. Facts can be verified (as objectively true or false) and are often presented in a straightforward fashion without emotion. Opinions are beliefs or judgments that are subjective in nature and sometimes presented with emotion.

Opinions use language that evaluates an idea and explains what the writer thinks about the idea. Opinion statements often use adjectives that carry positive or negative meanings. For example, when someone talks about a "brilliant career," this is an opinion because it can be disputed; there is no accepted, objective definition of "brilliant career." Signal words such as "should" and "ought" often indicate that the author is expressing an opinion.

Here is the way in which fact and opinion questions are usually asked:

- Which sentence in the passage is an expression of opinion rather than a statement of fact?

Expert tips:

- Remember that facts are things or events that can be observed, measured, or documented, such as dates or numbers. For example, the statement "In 1982 Anna rose to the position of plant manager" is a statement that can be confirmed by the company's records or Anna's coworkers.

- Opinions can be disputed. For example, the statement "Anna deserved more recognition for her work as a plant manager than she received" relies on a subjective judgment. It also can be disagreed with; someone else could make the claim that Anna was not an effective plant manager, or that Anna received enough recognition.

- Look out for qualifying words such as "probably" or "perhaps," statements of emotion or feeling such as "feel" or "believe," or comparison words such as "best" or "worst." The use of such words often indicates that the author is stating an opinion.

 Let's Try It!

Susan B. Anthony (1820-1906) fought against slavery until it was abolished in the mid-
Line   1860's. Then Anthony expanded her goal to include improving the status of all American women.
She spent the second half of her life devoted to that cause. Anthony spoke around the country for a woman's right to own property and to vote in state and national elections. She should be
5   considered the most influential figure in women's struggle for the right to vote and run for public office.

---

7. Which sentence is an expression of opinion rather than a statement of fact?

   (A) "Susan B. Anthony . . . the mid-1860's" (lines 1–2)
   (B) "She spent . . . that cause" (line 3)
   (C) "Anthony spoke . . . national elections" (lines 3–4)
   (D) "She should . . . public office" (lines 4–6)

Answer

Remember that opinions give either positive or negative evaluations of the subject of the passage. Answers (A), (B), and (C) provide information about Susan B. Anthony's life; these facts cannot be disputed. Also, these sentences do not tell us how to think about her. Answer (D), however, uses a comparison; the author urges the reader to think of Anthony as "the most influential figure." The author is asserting his or her own evaluative opinion; someone who claims that Susan B. Anthony was not an influential figure could dispute this opinion. Therefore, the correct answer is (D).

7 Interpreting graphic text

Some questions ask you about information presented as graphic text, such as tables, diagrams, charts, or graphs. These questions test your ability to understand information that is offered in a visual or spatial form.

Often the key to answering questions about tables, diagrams, charts, and graphs is to figure out how the information is organized. Pie charts, for example, are often used to show the relation of parts to a whole. Bar graphs are used to compare amounts. Tables of contents and indexes indicate how ideas are related through headings and subheadings.

Often a graphic text contains a *legend*, a key to explain the use of special shading, symbols, patterns, or shapes used in the graphic text. For example, a map might use three different colors to indicate three different temperature ranges for a particular geographical region. To understand what it means for a portion of the map to have a particular color, you would need to consult the legend. The legend is usually in a box or otherwise set off from the rest of the graphic text.

Most of these questions ask you to do one of two things. One kind of question asks you to find specific information using the graphic text provided. The other kind asks you to describe how the information is organized.

Here are the ways in which graphic text questions are usually asked:

- What conclusion can be drawn from the data presented in the graph?

- According to the chart, X is larger than . . .

- On which page would you find X?

- The table of contents is organized by . . .

Expert tips:

- Familiarize yourself with the most common forms of graphic text, such as pie charts, line and bar graphs, tables of contents, and indexes.

- Be conscious of how the information is arranged spatially. For example, in indexes and tables of contents, learn to distinguish between headings and subheadings. Often subheadings are indented more than main headings.

- Pay close attention to the title of the graphic text. This provides valuable information about how information is organized, such as through direct comparison or relationships between part and whole. For example, a title for a bar graph such as "Voter Participation, 1920–2000" suggests that numbers or percentages of voter participation are compared across years.

- Look closely at the *legend* and the labels for specific parts of the graphic text. These can help guide you when the question asks for detailed information.

- Don't choose an answer just because it appears on the chart, graph, or table. Often all of the choices appear in the graphic text. Make sure the answer you choose applies to the particular question.

Let's Try It!

Questions 8–9 are based on the following excerpt from an index.

> Abell, Bennett and Elizabeth, 37
> Abolitionism
> British, 438
> Clay and, 269. See also Clay, H.,
> on slavery.
> increases evils of slavery, 18
> and Missouri Compromise, 337
> Republicans and, 577-589. See
> also Republican Party: and
> slavery.
> Abolitionism, Abraham Lincoln on,
> 497

8. On which page or pages would a person be most likely to find information on abolitionism outside of the United States?

   (A) 269
   (B) 337
   (C) 438
   (D) 497

Answer

This question asks you to identify a subheading within a larger category. First identify the main category—Abolitionism. Then identify the subheading that corresponds to the specific information being asked. The only subheading that refers to a topic not related to the United States is "British" on page 438. Therefore, the correct answer is (C).

9. After looking at pages 577–589, where could a person go to find additional information on abolitionism and the Republican Party, according to the index?

   (A) Under "Slavery" in the index
   (B) Under "Republican Party: and slavery" in the index
   (C) In another volume devoted to the Missouri Compromise
   (D) In another volume devoted to Abraham Lincoln

Answer

This question requires you to acknowledge the intersection of two topics, Abolitionism and the Republican Party. The answer must include both of these elements. Answers (A), (C), and (D) do not contain both elements. Only the answer (B) both is under the heading of "Abolitionism" and specifically refers to the Republican Party.

You will find more sample questions as part of the complete practice test in chapter 7.

Part II: Application of Reading Skills and Knowledge to Classroom Instruction

Reading Application questions are typically based on classroom scenarios in which students are involved in reading-related tasks. Examples of such tasks include understanding important ideas in assigned reading passages or working on vocabulary development.

The Reading Application questions draw on many of the skills tested in the Reading Skills section, but they ask you to apply those skills in a classroom context. For example, while a Reading Skills question might measure your understanding of a reading passage by asking you to identify the main idea of the passage, a Reading Application question might ask you to identify which question would be the best one to pose to a student to find out whether the student understands the main idea. The Reading Application questions also test skills and knowledge important to assisting in classroom instruction, including the ability to understand directions, alphabetize words, and help students use a dictionary.

What's Being Tested?

Some Reading Application questions concern *foundations of reading*: the knowledge and skills that students need when they are learning the basic features of words and written text. These questions measure your ability to help students

- sound out words (e.g., long and short vowels, consonant sounds, rhymes)

- break down words into parts (e.g., recognize syllables, root words, prefixes, suffixes)

- decode words or phrases using context clues

- distinguish between synonyms, antonyms, and homonyms

- alphabetize words

Other Reading Application questions concern *tools of the reading process*: the common strategies you may use in the classroom before, during, and after reading to aid students' reading skills. These questions measure your ability to

- help students use prereading strategies, such as skimming or making predictions

- ask questions about a reading selection to help students understand the selection

- make accurate observations about students' ability to understand and interpret text

- help students use a dictionary

- interpret written directions

As with the Reading Skills and Knowledge questions, the Reading Application questions often involve reading passages. These passages are typical of the kinds of reading passages assigned to students in the classroom. Some passages are accompanied by two or more questions; others are accompanied by only one question. A group of questions for one passage might contain questions concerning both the foundations of reading and the tools of the reading process.

Following is a review course to help you review the knowledge and skills you will need to do well on the Reading Application questions. The review course is followed by sample questions.

REVIEW COURSE: Reading Application

1 Foundations of Reading

If you are already working with students in the classroom, you are probably familiar with the skills and knowledge covered in foundations of reading questions. If you are not yet in the classroom, or if you work with older students, you may want to remind yourself about some of the following knowledge and skills for helping younger students become strong readers.

- **Sounding out words**

  Sounding out words helps students to recognize words and use them correctly in spoken and written English. Words can be sounded out in several ways, including:

  By vowel sounds:

  ➤ Review the vowels of the English language: *a, e, i, o, u,* and sometimes *y.*

  ➤ Review the difference between long and short vowel sounds. For example, the word *cap* has a short vowel sound (*căp*), while the word *cape* has a long vowel sound (*cāpe*). The silent *e* at the end of the word signals the long vowel sound.

    Note: The pronunciation of vowel sounds is represented in written text using symbols like the ones above. You have probably seen these symbols in dictionary entries to explain the correct pronunciation of a word. Sometimes these symbols may appear in *ParaPro Assessment* questions. Although your knowledge of these symbols will not be tested directly, you should be prepared to encounter some of the more common pronunciation symbols for vowels. These include: *cāke, līke, nōte* (long vowel sound) and *căt, lĭt, nŏt* (short vowel sound).

  ➤ Review common vowel combinations like *oo, ou, ai, ie, ea,* and *eigh.*

By consonant sounds:

> ➤ Know the consonants of the English language.

> ➤ Review the sounds of consonants, especially those consonants whose sound can change or consonants that have similar sounds. For example, *s* sometimes sounds like *z* (as in the word *rise*) but at other times has a softer sound (as in *sack*); *c* can have a hard sound at the beginning of a word (*cast*), but can sound like *s* when used within a word (*rice*).

> ➤ Review common consonant combinations, such as *th*, *sh*, *gh*, *-ct*, *-ck*, *sl-*, and *tr-*.

You should also be able to apply your knowledge of vowel and consonant sounds to the principle of rhyming. Rhyming words are two or more words that share the same end sound. *Dog* and *frog* are rhymes because they share the end sound of *-og*. Watch out for words that share the same end spelling but have different pronunciations, such as *bough* and *rough*. These words are not rhymes because they are pronounced differently.

- **Breaking down words into parts**

    Sometimes students can better understand a word by breaking down the word into parts. By examining the word's root, prefix, or suffix, students can infer the meaning of the word. Students may also need to understand compound words and break down words into syllables. Review the following definitions and examples of word parts:

    Prefixes:

    Prefixes are groups of letters added to the beginning of a word to change its meaning. Common prefixes include *pre-*, *post-*, *micro-*, and *un-*, among others. Prefixes often carry meanings of their own; for example, the prefix *pre-* means "before"; to "preview" something is to view it before others do. You should be able to identify the prefixes of common words. Here are some examples of words that begin with prefixes:

Prefix	Meaning	Examples
anti-	against	antidote, antibody
mal-	wrong	malformed, malign
non-	not	nonsense, nonentity
post-	after	postwar, postscript

Suffixes:

Suffixes are groups of letters placed at the end of a word to change its meaning. Common suffixes include: *-ly*, *-ate*, and *-er*, among others. Suffixes often change the form of the word; for example, adding *-ly* can change an adjective to an adverb (e.g., *sad* becomes *sadly*). You should be able to identify the suffixes of common words. Here are some examples of words that end with suffixes:

Suffix	Meaning	Examples
-acy	state or quality	candidacy, privacy
-ment	condition of	fulfillment, payment
-ize	cause to become	privatize, realize
-less	without	humorless, senseless

Root words:

A root is what is left of a word once its prefixes and suffixes have been removed. Many words share the same root. For example, the words *transport* and *portable* have the same root word, *port* (meaning to carry). The root word helps determine the meaning of the word. Root words in English are often Greek, Latin, or Germanic in origin. Here are common roots in English:

Root	Meaning	Examples
-audi-	to hear	audience, audible
-manu-	hand	manual, manipulate
-sent-	to feel	sentiment, resent
-vac-	empty	vacant, vacuum

Compound words:

Compound words are single words made by putting two whole words together. Examples of common compound words include *catfish*, *starship*, *doghouse*, and *buttermilk*. Students are often taught to break down a compound word into its component parts to understand the compound word's meaning.

Syllables:

When a word is broken down into syllables, it is broken down into distinct units of sound. Students may learn how to break down written words into syllables to help them pronounce the words aloud. Breaking words down into syllables may also help students with spelling and with recognizing the different parts of a word (such as prefixes and suffixes, described on previous pages). When words with double consonants, such as the double *tt* in the word *motto*, are broken down into syllables, the two consonants are often divided: *mot* | *to*.

You can find out the syllables for different words by looking them up in the dictionary. Here are a few examples of words divided into syllables:

ob | ser | va | tion
play | ing
trav | el | ing

- **Decoding the meanings of words from context**

When students encounter a difficult word in a passage they are reading, they can either apply some of the strategies above for sounding out or breaking down the word into parts or try to decode the word using contextual clues. This involves looking for clues within the sentence or passage that may indicate the meaning of the word. Many of the strategies for understanding vocabulary in context that you used in the Reading Skills and Knowledge questions work for the Reading Application section. Strategies for defining words from context include the following:

➤ Look for synonyms or other examples of the word in the passage. Sometimes a passage uses several different words for the same thing. For example, in the sentence, "The unusual decorations in Jane's living room reflect her eccentric tastes," students could infer that eccentric means "not ordinary" because of the synonym "unusual" in the first half of the sentence.

➤ Look for words with opposite meanings. Sometimes a sentence sets up a contrast between two things. A student can figure out the meaning of an unknown word by understanding it as the opposite of a word the student already knows. For example, in the sentence, "Instead of being clear and straightforward, the governor's speech was very convoluted," a student could understand the meaning of "convoluted" by understanding it as opposite to "clear and straightforward."

- **Synonyms, antonyms, and homonyms**

Students can increase their understanding of words and the variety of words they use in speaking and writing by understanding synonyms, antonyms, and homonyms.

Synonyms: Synonyms are words that have similar meanings. Here are some examples of synonyms:

close	and	*near*
angry	and	*mad*
happy	and	*glad*

Antonyms: Antonyms are words that have opposite meanings. Here are some examples of antonyms:

new	and	*old*
short	and	*tall*
clean	and	*dirty*

Homonyms: Homonyms are words that sound alike but have different meanings. Here are some examples of homonyms:

eye	and	*I*
piece	and	*peace*
way	and	*weigh*

- **Alphabetizing words**

Knowing how to alphabetize is a key organizing strategy for students. It is also a common strategy used by teachers and paraprofessionals to keep the classroom organized.

Alphabetize words according to the order in which the letters appear in the words. Work methodically from the first letter to the last (usually, you need to look at only the first two or three letters to alphabetize words). Sometimes it is easiest to alphabetize words when they are listed directly underneath each other, as follows:

Before alphabetizing:

crow
crane
cross
crook

After alphabetizing:

crane
crook
cross
crow

2 Tools of the Reading Process

Paraprofessionals use a variety of strategies when they assist in the instruction of reading. For example, they may need to ask students questions about a reading passage to determine how well the students understand the passage, evaluate informally students' responses about a passage, or help students look up unfamiliar words in the dictionary. Paraprofessionals may also need to help implement activities designed by the teacher, so they need to be able to understand and follow directions and to help students do the same. It may be helpful to review some of the basic skills and knowledge needed for these tasks.

- **Evaluating appropriate student responses**

  One strategy you may need to use is the ability to evaluate how well students understand what they read. This skill draws on your own ability to understand what you read; to do this, you need to use the kinds of skills you learned in the Reading Skills and Knowledge section. For example, you may need to identify the main idea or supporting idea in a passage, or you may need to make inferences about a passage or identify how it is organized. Once you understand these things yourself, you will be able to evaluate how well students understand them. However, you should keep in mind that students may not paraphrase a main idea or describe an organizational pattern exactly as you do.

- **Asking a question to help students understand a passage**

  Another important reading strategy used by students, teachers, and paraprofessionals alike is the strategy of asking questions. Often, a paraprofessional working one-on-one with a student will need to ask the student questions about a reading passage. This helps determine how well the student understands the passage. It can also help the student understand the passage by directing the student's attention to key aspects of the passage, because in searching for the answer to the question, the student must focus on important parts of the passage. A good question is specific and direct; it should also concern important aspects of the passage.

- **Helping students to use a dictionary**

  Students (and all readers) often need to use a dictionary to look up unfamiliar words. Because some words have multiple meanings, students may need help determining which meaning is most appropriate for a word in a given context. You should be familiar with the skill of selecting an appropriate dictionary definition for a word in a particular context.

  For example, a student may wish to look up the word "bristle" after encountering the word in the sentence "Devin bristled when Louis insulted him." But upon looking up the word in the dictionary, the student finds several definitions:

  1. (noun) A stiff hair
  2. (verb) To stand stiffly on end like bristles

3. (verb) To raise the bristles
4. (verb) To react in an angry or offended manner
5. (verb) To be covered with or as if with bristles

To help the student choose the appropriate definition, you need to use each definition of the word in the sentence and choose the definition that makes the most sense *in the context of the sentence*. In the example above, definition 4 fits because it would make sense for Devin "to react in an angry or offended manner" when he has been insulted.

■ **Interpreting directions and/or helping students to interpret directions**

Often a paraprofessional will help implement an activity designed by the teacher. The teacher may have special directions for the paraprofessional to follow during the activity, or the paraprofessional may need to help students follow directions from the teacher. Following directions draws on the ability to read carefully. To read directions carefully, pay attention to *who, what,* and *when: who* is supposed to perform an action, *what* the person is supposed to do, and *when* the person should perform that action. In a classroom context, directions are often in steps, so you need to watch for words like "first," "next," and "then" to know *when* to do something.

Answering the Reading Application Questions

Now that you have reviewed common skills and knowledge used to assist in the instruction of reading, you are ready to explore how these skills and knowledge are tested in actual questions in the *ParaPro Assessment*.

Here are some ways in which foundations of reading questions are usually asked:

■ What would be an effective strategy the paraprofessional could use to help the student understand the word X?

■ Which word from the story is the clearest example of a word with a Y sound?

■ Which word from the passage is a compound word?

■ Which pair of words is a pair of antonyms (synonyms, homonyms)?

■ How should the words be arranged so that they are in alphabetical order?

Here are some ways in which tools of the reading process questions are usually asked:

■ Which response from the students is most accurate?

■ Which response from the students shows the best understanding of the clues?

■ What question could the paraprofessional ask the students that would help them understand Z?

■ Students are asked to put the events in the order in which they happened. What is the correct order?

■ According to the assignment, the first (second, last) task the student should do is . . .

■ Which definition should the student use to understand the word Q in the context of the sentence?

 Let's Try It!

It's time to work through some sample questions using the skills and strategies you have learned above.

Questions 10–11 are based on the following passage from a book students are reading in class.

Camping Close to Home
Chapter 1: Getting Ready

Cindy took a careful look at her checklist. Her brother and sister were taking her camping. She had everything she needed piled on the kitchen floor. She'd even found the compass she had bought at the Grand Canyon last year.

"What if I get hungry?" she asked Ryan.
"We're bringing lots of food," he said.
"But what if we run out?" she asked.
"Then I'll come back to the kitchen."
"Promise?" Cindy asked as she stuffed a candy bar into her purple backpack.
"I promise," Ryan said.

Just then, Alice dashed in through the back door. "Okay, I've got the tent set up," she said.
"Did you stake it down?" Ryan asked.
"Absolutely," Alice said. "It's not going anywhere."
"But we are," Cindy said.
"We sure are," Ryan said. "So let's get started."

Laughing, Cindy followed him out to the backyard.

10. Students are learning how to make predictions about a story by using clues from the title of the story, the chapter headings, and what happens in the story itself. The paraprofessional asks students where Cindy will be camping. Which response from the students shows the best understanding of the clues?

    (A) Cindy is going to camp at the Grand Canyon.
    (B) Cindy is going to camp at a campground.
    (C) Cindy is going to camp in her backyard.
    (D) Cindy is going to camp in the Rocky Mountains.

Answer

This question addresses an important prereading strategy: the ability to make predictions. To predict what happens next in the story, you need to use context clues such as titles, chapter headings, and what happens in the story itself. Begin by looking at the title of the story, "Camping Close to Home." This title suggests that Cindy will not be going far from her house. Next, look for details in the story that provide further clues about where Cindy will be camping. For example, the fact that Alice has already set up the tent suggests that the tent is very close by. In addition, Ryan's statement that he'll "come back to the kitchen" if they run out of food also implies that they will be camping very close by. This is further supported by the concluding sentence of the passage: "Laughing, Cindy followed him out to the backyard." Thus, choice (C), "Cindy is going to camp in her backyard," is the correct answer.

11. Students are learning about compound words (words made up of two or more whole words joined together). Which word from the story is a compound word?

    (A) camping
    (B) checklist
    (C) compass
    (D) kitchen

Answer

Remember that a compound word is a word that is made from joining together two whole words. Only answer (B), *checklist*, can be separated into two whole words: check and list. (A), *camping* has a suffix, *-ing*, but that is not a complete word. Therefore, the correct answer is (B), *checklist*.

Questions 12–14 are based on the following passage from a textbook that students are reading in small groups.

Line

5

People have long known that food spoils at warm temperatures but not at cold temperatures. In fact, in 1626 an English scientist, Sir Francis Bacon, successfully preserved a chicken by stuffing it with snow. But the reason food spoils was not understood until after 1683, when the microscope was invented. For the first time scientists could see tiny living creatures—bacteria and molds—that we call microbes. Some microbes are helpful, but others are harmful. Most are killed by very hot temperatures, multiply rapidly in warm temperatures, and do not multiply much in cold temperatures.

12. The paraprofessional asks the students why the author mentions Sir Francis Bacon. Which response from the students is most accurate?

(A) To explain why food spoils at warm temperatures

(B) To indicate when microbes, such as bacteria and molds, were first discovered

(C) To provide an example of the kinds of food that were eaten in England in the 1600's

(D) To support the claim that people had long known that food does not spoil at cold temperatures

Answer

The goal of the paraprofessional's question is to help students understand how a detail fits into the overall organization of the passage. To confirm which student response is most accurate, the paraprofessional must determine what role the mention of Bacon plays in the author's discussion of food preservation and microbes. To make that determination, look at the sentence in which Bacon's name appears and at the sentences before and after that to understand the full context in which Bacon is brought up. The sentence in which Bacon appears is preceded by the assertion that people had long known that food doesn't spoil at cold temperatures. The author goes on to provide an example of a particular person— Sir Frances Bacon—who had this knowledge in 1626: Bacon stuffed the chicken with snow because he knew it would be preserved by cold temperatures. Thus the best answer is (D): the example of Sir Frances Bacon supports the claim that people had long known that food does not spoil at cold temperatures.

13. What question could the paraprofessional ask the students that would help them understand why food spoils at warm temperatures?

    (A) How do people benefit from helpful microbes?
    (B) What happens to bacteria and molds at different temperatures?
    (C) Why are some foods cooked and others eaten raw?
    (D) When did people first know that food could be preserved at cold temperatures?

Answer

To help the students understand why food spoils at warm temperatures, you must pick the answer choice that directs their attention to this discussion in the passage. Only choice (B) leads the students to this information. The passage indicates that food spoils because microbes (bacteria and molds) multiply at warm temperatures. At very hot temperatures, microbes are killed, and at very cold temperatures, they do not multiply much at all. Choice (A) is incorrect both because the passage does not contain the information to answer this question and because information about helpful microbes would not help students understand why food spoils. Choices (C) and (D) are incorrect because they do not draw students' attention to the place in the passage that indicates how food spoils.

14. A paraprofessional is working with a student who is having trouble understanding the word "microbes" (line 5). What would be the most effective strategy the paraprofessional could use to help the student understand those words?

    (A) Have the student research the time period during which the microscope was invented.
    (B) Encourage the student to sound out the word and practice spelling it out loud.
    (C) Ask the student what purpose the phrase "tiny living creatures" (line 4) serves in the passage.
    (D) Suggest that the student reread the first sentence to find clues about the meaning of the word.

Answer

The goal of the question is to help the student find the meaning of the word. Choice (A) can be eliminated because it has the student research a historical time period, a task that does not focus the student's attention on the meaning of "microbes." Choice (B) can be eliminated because sounding out and spelling do not provide information about the meaning of the word. Choice (D) can be eliminated because the first sentence of the passage does not contain any reference to microbes; thus there are no contextual clues for the student to use to define the term. Only answer (C) directs the student's attention to the definition of "microbes" that is provided in the phrase "tiny living creatures"; therefore, the correct answer is (C).

You will find more sample questions as part of the complete practice test in chapter 7.

Chapter 5
Math Review Course with Sample Questions

► ► ► ► ► ► ► ► ► ► ► ►

Overview

The 30 questions in the math section of the *ParaPro Assessment* fall into two categories:

I. Math Skills and Knowledge (approximately 18 questions)

II. Application of Math Skills and Knowledge to Classroom Instruction (approximately 12 questions)

All of the questions are multiple-choice. Each of the questions or incomplete statements in the section is followed by four suggested answers or completions. All of the questions involve mathematical skills commonly taught at the elementary, middle, and high school level. The questions also address common uses of math skills in everyday life. You will not need any advanced training in mathematics in order to answer these questions.

The first category of questions tests your general math skills and knowledge. These questions may look familiar to you, since they are similar to math questions you may have encountered on other multiple-choice tests. Skills and knowledge that will be tested include addition, subtraction, multiplication, and division of whole numbers, fractions, and decimals; basic algebra; geometry; measurement; and the interpretation of numerical data from tables, charts, and graphs.

The second category of questions tests your ability to *apply* your math skills and knowledge to classroom instruction. These questions look slightly different from questions you may have seen on other tests because they present an actual classroom situation or activity. To answer the questions you need only to apply your math knowledge and skills. You do *not* need specialized knowledge of philosophies or approaches to teaching math in order to answer the questions.

You may not use a calculator.

Part I: The Math Skills and Knowledge Section

The Math Skills and Knowledge questions assess your knowledge of mathematical concepts and your ability to apply them to abstract and real-life situations. Below is a brief review of the mathematical concepts and symbols with which you should be familiar before you take the *ParaPro Assessment*.

Mathematical concepts

Don't worry if you don't know all of these concepts and symbols. They will be explained in much more detail on the following pages.

Arithmetic:

■ How and when to add, subtract, multiply, and divide whole numbers, fractions, and decimals

■ How to order and compare whole numbers, fractions, and decimals

■ How to determine place value

■ How to use exponents

■ How to read and calculate percents

■ How to identify odd and even numbers

■ How to distinguish prime numbers and numbers that are divisible

■ Estimation

Algebra:

■ How to identify and use negative numbers

■ How to express and interpret relationships using variables, including formulas and simple equations

Geometry:

■ How to identify basic geometric shapes, such as rectangles, cubes and special triangles (isosceles, equilateral, right)

■ How to locate points on a coordinate grid

Measurement:

■ How to convert between units or measures in the same system

■ How to represent time and energy

■ How to measure perimeters, areas, and volumes of common figures (triangles, circles, cubes, etc.)

Data Organization and Interpretation:

■ How to interpret and create graphs, tables, and other visual displays of data

■ How to compute mean, median, and mode

Expert tip:

- Review each point of the mathematical topics above. Mark any topics that seem unfamiliar to you and focus your energy on reviewing these concepts in the Review Course.

REVIEW COURSE: Math

This brief course reviews the mathematical vocabulary and processes that you may encounter in the classroom. This review course focuses on defining mathematical terms and concepts as well as specific problem-solving techniques. Because paraprofessionals will be helping students to learn such concepts, the emphasis of this review course is on the *steps* necessary to recognize and solve problems.

Use this course to familiarize yourself with the kinds of mathematical vocabulary and concepts you will see on the *ParaPro Assessment*. After you have worked through the sample questions and/or the practice test, you should revisit the review course to clarify your understanding of any types of problems you may have had difficulty with.

Mathematical Vocabulary: Words and Phrases You Should Know

- Integers: Integers are numbers that are not fractions or decimals; they can be either positive or negative. For example, −3, −2, −1, 0, 1, 2, and 3 are all integers.

- Positive Integers: Positive integers are integers to the right of zero on the number line (1, 2, 3, 4, ...). Positive integers are also called whole numbers.

- Negative Integers: Negative integers are integers to the left of zero on the number line (−1, −2, −3, −4, ...)

- Odd numbers: An odd number is any integer <u>*not*</u> *divisible by 2* (±1, ±3, ±5, ±7, ...)

- Even numbers: An even number is any integer *divisible by 2* (0, ±2, ±4, ±6, ...)

- Consecutive integers: Consecutive integers are integers in a sequence, such as 1, 2, 3 or −1, 0, 1.

- Prime numbers: A prime number is an integer that can be divided only by 1 and itself; it has no other divisor. For example, 2, 3, 5, 7, 11, and 13 are all prime numbers. (1 is not a prime number.)

- Factor: A factor is a divisor of an integer. For example, 1, 3, 5, and 15 are factors of 15 because you can divide 15 by any of these numbers and the result will be an integer (−1, −3, −5, and −15 are also factors of 15). However, 2 is not a factor of 15 because 15 ÷ 2 = 7.5 (not an integer). Zero (0) is not a factor of any integer.

- Multiple: A multiple of an integer is the product of that integer and another integer. For example, some multiples of 4 are −8, −4, 0, 4, 8, 12, and 16. However, 2 is not a multiple of 4; it is a factor of 4. Zero (0) is a multiple of every integer.

A Quick Reference Guide to Mathematical Symbols

When you see a mathematical symbol, it is standing in for a particular phrase. The following are some common mathematical symbols and the phrases they stand in for.

$=$ is equal to
$\neq$ is not equal to
$<$ is less than
$>$ is greater than
$\leq$ is less than or equal to
$\geq$ is greater than or equal to

1 Arithmetic and Basic Algebra

Integers

Integers include positive whole numbers, their negatives, and zero (0).

Integers can be represented on a number line as follows:

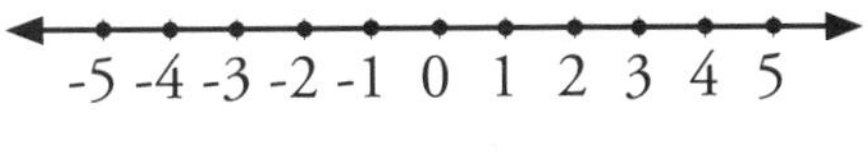

The number line above provides a visual comparison of the relationship between numbers. As you move left on the number line, the number values get smaller; as you move right on the number line, the number values get larger. Use the terms *greater than* (>), *less than* (<), *equal to* (=) and *between* when comparing numbers.

Example:

Two is greater than negative three: $2 > -3$

Negative four is less than negative two: $-4 < -2$

Negative one is between negative three and zero: $-3 < -1 < 0$

Ordering Whole Numbers

Whole numbers are positive integers you use to count or tell how many. Whole numbers *never* contain fractions or decimals (e.g., $\frac{1}{2}$ and 0.3 are not whole numbers).

Whole numbers can be represented on a number line as follows:

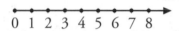

As with the number line for integers, the number line for whole numbers provides a visual comparison of the relationship between numbers.

Examples:

Five is greater than three: 5 > 3
Two is less than four: 2 < 4
Three plus three is equal to six: 3 + 3 = 6
Five is between four and six: 4 < 5 < 6

Place Value

0, 1, 2, 3, 4, 5, 6, 7, 8, and 9 are called *digits*, and they are used in combination to represent numbers. For example, the number 25 is composed of the digits 2 and 5. Each digit in a number carries a value depending upon the place it occupies in the number. Below is a chart of place values for the number 2,463,587:

Millions	Hundred Thousands	Ten Thousands	Thousands	Hundreds	Tens	Ones
2	4	6	3	5	8	7

Each number carries the value of its place. For example, the value of the 2 is 2,000,000. The 2 is in the millions place. The value of the 8 is 80. The 8 is in the tens place. If you read the number out loud, you would say two million, four hundred sixty-three thousand, five hundred eighty-seven.

Computing Whole Numbers: Addition, Subtraction, Multiplication, and Division

Addition

Add whole numbers by adding the digits of the same place value, and so on, starting with the ones place and moving left towards the tens, hundreds, thousands and so on.

Example: Add: 423 + 145

First, align the digits according to place:
$$\begin{array}{r} 423 \\ +145 \end{array}$$

Then add each column of digits:
$$\begin{array}{r} 423 \\ +145 \\ \hline 568 \end{array}$$

Carrying: Sometimes when you add a column of digits, such as shown below, the sum will be 10 or more. In the following example, you carry the 1 to the next column.

Example: Add: 5,098 + 2,767

First, align the digits according to place:
$$\begin{array}{r} 5,098 \\ +2,767 \end{array}$$

Then add:
$$\begin{array}{r} {\scriptstyle 1\ 1} \\ 5,098 \\ +2,767 \\ \hline 7,865 \end{array}$$

The sum of the digits in the ones place is 15. The 5 is left in the ones place and the 1 is carried over to the tens place. The sum of the digits in the tens place is $1 + 9 + 6 = 16$. The 6 is left in the tens place and the 1 is carried to the hundreds place. The sum of the digits in the hundreds place is $1 + 0 + 7 = 8$. You do not have to carry anything to the thousands column.

Subtraction

Subtract whole numbers by subtracting the digits of the same place value, and so on, starting with the ones place and moving left towards the tens, hundreds, thousands and so on.

Example: Subtract: 589 − 237

First, align the digits according to place:
$$\begin{array}{r} 589 \\ -237 \end{array}$$

Then subtract each column of digits:
$$\begin{array}{r} 589 \\ -237 \\ \hline 352 \end{array}$$

Borrowing: Sometimes when you subtract the digits in a column, the result is negative. When this happens, you borrow from the next column in order to ensure that the result remains positive.

Example: Subtract: 962 − 527

First, align the digits according to place:
$$\begin{array}{r} 962 \\ -527 \end{array}$$

Then subtract:
$$\begin{array}{r} {\scriptstyle 5\ 12} \\ 96\!\!\!/2 \\ -527 \\ \hline 435 \end{array}$$

The difference of the digits in the ones place is negative ($2 - 7 = -5$). You borrow a "1" from the tens place, which requires you to subtract 1 from the number in the tens place ($6 - 1 = 5$); the number in the tens place is now 5. The number in the ones place is now 12. $12 - 7 = 5$; 5 is the result in the ones place. You then subtract the rest of the columns of digits (tens place: $5 - 2 = 3$; hundreds place: $9 - 5 = 4$). The answer is 435.

Multiplication

Multiplication is adding a number to itself a given number of times.

For example, $2 \times 3 = 3 + 3 = 6$

When multiplying whole numbers greater than nine, you may need to use a process that involves finding *partial products* and adding them together to get the final answer. The partial product is formed when you multiply a number and each digit of the other number in a problem.

Example: Multiply: 124×15

First, align the digits:
$$\begin{array}{r} 124 \\ \times 15 \\ \hline \end{array}$$

Then multiply to find the partial products:
$$\begin{array}{r} 124 \\ \times 15 \\ \hline 620 \\ 124 \\ \hline \end{array}$$

When finding partial products, always begin with the ones place ($124 \times 5 = 620$). Align the last digit of the answer with the place for which you are finding the partial product (thus the 0 in 620 is aligned with the ones place; the 4 in 124 is aligned with the tens place).

Then add the partial products:
$$\begin{array}{r} 124 \\ \times 15 \\ \hline 620 \\ 124 \\ \hline 1,860 \end{array}$$

The answer is 1,860.

Division

Division is finding the number of times a given number (the *divisor*) can be subtracted from another number.

For example, $12 \div 3 = 4$ because 3 can be subtracted from 12 four times ($12 - 3 = 9$; $9 - 3 = 6$; $6 - 3 = 3$; $3 - 3 = 0$).

Sometimes a number cannot be divided evenly by another number. When this happens, the extra amount is called the *remainder*. The remainder is always less than the divisor.

Example: Divide: $681 \div 12$

$$\begin{array}{r} 56 \\ 12\overline{)681} \\ -60 \\ \hline 81 \\ -72 \\ \hline 9 \text{ (remainder)} \end{array}$$

The answer is 56 remainder 9 (56 R9).

Exponents

Exponents are used to indicate repeated multiplication. The exponent signifies the number of times a base number is multiplied by itself.

Example:

Exponent

$$3^4 = 3 \times 3 \times 3 \times 3 = 81$$

Base

Order of Operations

Sometimes you will be asked to solve problems that ask you to perform a variety of operations (addition, multiplication, etc.). The order in which you perform these operations can affect the solution. Therefore, there is a standard order in which operations are performed:

1: **P**arentheses

2: **E**xponents

3: Do any **M**ultiplications or **D**ivisions in the order in which they occur, working from left to right.

4: Do any **A**dditions or **S**ubtractions in the order in which they occur, working from left to right.

Example: Solve the following problem: $2^3 + 6 \times (9 - 4) \div 2$

Solve what is in the parentheses first: $9 - 4 = 5$; result: $2^3 + 6 \times 5 \div 2$

Then solve the term with exponents: $2^3 = 8$; result: $8 + 6 \times 5 \div 2$

Then multiply: $6 \times 5 = 30$; result: $8 + 30 \div 2$

Then divide: $30 \div 2 = 15$; result: $8 + 15$

Then add: $8 + 15 = 23$.

Decimals

Numbers between 0 and 1 are represented by decimals. For example, 0.3 is between 0 and 1. You can see a visual representation of decimals on the number line below.

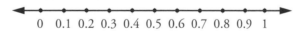

$$0 \quad 0.1 \quad 0.2 \quad 0.3 \quad 0.4 \quad 0.5 \quad 0.6 \quad 0.7 \quad 0.8 \quad 0.9 \quad 1$$

Like whole numbers, decimals also have place values. Below is a chart of decimal place values for the decimal 0.2597.

Ones	.	Tenths	Hundredths	Thousandths	Ten Thousandths
0	.	2	5	9	7

The value of 2 is two-tenths; the 2 is in the tenths place. The value of 9 is nine-thousandths; 9 is in the thousandths place.

Compare the value of two decimals by comparing the values of the digits in each place, beginning with the tenths place and moving to the right:

Adding zeros to the right of the last digit of a decimal does not change the value. The decimals 0.350 and 0.3500 are equivalent to 0.35 and each other.

Examples:

- 0.235 < 0.297 (The numbers in the tenths place are the same, but the values in the hundredths place are different: 3 < 9.)

- 0.235 > 0.178 (The numbers in the tenths place are different; 2 > 1.)

- 0.35 < 0.355 (The numbers in the tenths place are the same, but read 0.35 as 0.350; 0 < 5.)

Computation with decimals

Addition, subtraction, multiplication, and division of decimals works much the same way as with whole numbers, except that you must pay close attention to the placement of the decimal.

Addition: Add decimals by adding the digits of the same place value. Make sure that you line up the decimal points.

Example: Add: 2.572 + 10.34

First, align the digits according to place, placing a zero in the thousandths place for 10.34:

$$\begin{array}{r} 2.572 \\ +10.340 \end{array}$$

Then add each column of digits:

$$\begin{array}{r} 2.\overset{1}{5}72 \\ +10.340 \\ \hline 12.912 \end{array}$$

Subtraction: Subtract decimals by subtracting the digits of the same place value. Make sure that you line up the decimal points.

Example: Subtract: 5.32 − 3.716

First, align the digits:

$$\begin{array}{r} 5.320 \\ -3.716 \end{array}$$

Then subtract:

$$\begin{array}{r} \overset{4}{5}.\overset{13}{3}\overset{1}{2}\overset{10}{0} \\ -3.716 \\ \hline 1.604 \end{array}$$

Multiplication: You do not have to align the decimals in a multiplication problem; instead, align the factors by their final digits. Use the same steps to multiply decimals as you would for whole numbers. Then make sure you put the decimal point in the appropriate place using the following technique.

Step 1: Count the total number of decimal places in the factors.

Step 2: Starting to the right of the last number on the right, count off that number of decimal places and insert the decimal point.

Step 3: You may need to insert a zero in order to make enough places.

Example: Multiply: 0.015 × 2.37

First, align the digits:

$$\begin{array}{r} 2.37 \\ \times 0.015 \end{array}$$

Multiply to find the partial products:

$$\begin{array}{r} 2.37 \\ \times 0.015 \\ \hline 1185 \\ 237 \\ \hline 3555 \end{array}$$

Add the partial products. Then count the number of decimal places needed and adjust the answer accordingly:

$$\begin{array}{r} 2.37 \\ \times 0.015 \\ \hline 1185 \\ 237 \\ \hline .03555 \end{array}$$

Division: Before you begin dividing, move the decimal point to the right to make the divisor a whole number. Then move the decimal point in the dividend (the number being divided) the same number of places. Then divide, keeping the decimal point in the answer the same as in the new dividend.

Example: Divide: 2.24 ÷ 1.4

$$1.4\overline{)2.24}$$

$$\begin{array}{r} 1.6 \\ 14\overline{)22.4} \\ -14 \\ \hline 84 \\ -84 \\ \hline 0 \end{array}$$

So, 2.24 ÷ 1.4 = 1.6 (with 0 remainder)

Fractions

A fraction indicates a part of a whole. Fractions are composed of numerators and denominators. The denominator indicates the total number of parts that make up the whole. The numerator indicates the specific number of parts being identified.

$$\frac{2}{5} \begin{array}{l} - \text{ numerator} \\ - \text{ denominator} \end{array}$$

This fraction identifies 2 parts out of a total of 5 parts.

A mixed number is represented by a whole number and a fraction. For example, $3\frac{3}{5}$ is a mixed number.

An improper fraction is a fraction in which the numerator is greater than the denominator. For example, $\frac{7}{3}$ is an improper fraction.

Improper fractions can be changed into mixed numbers and vice versa. Here's how:

To change an improper fraction to a mixed number, divide the numerator by the denominator. Then put the remainder over the denominator as the fraction.

Example:

$$\frac{12}{5} = 12 \div 5 = 2R2 = 2\frac{2}{5}$$

To change a mixed number into an improper fraction, multiply the whole number by the denominator. Add the result to the numerator and place over the original denominator.

Example:

$$3\frac{2}{3} = \frac{(3\times3)+2}{3} = \frac{9+2}{3} = \frac{11}{3}$$

Equivalent fractions are two fractions with different numerators and denominators but that indicate equivalent amounts. You can find an equivalent fraction by multiplying the numerator and denominator by the same number or by dividing the numerator and the denominator by the same number. For example, $\frac{2}{3}$ and $\frac{14}{21}$ are equivalent fractions because:

$$\frac{2}{3} = \frac{(2\times7)}{(3\times7)} = \frac{14}{21}$$

Also, for example, $\frac{12}{15}$ and $\frac{4}{5}$ are equivalent fractions because:

$$\frac{12}{15} = \frac{(12\div3)}{(15\div3)} = \frac{4}{5}$$

Fractions can also be compared on a number line. As with whole numbers and decimals, use the words *equivalent to, greater than, less than,* and *between* to compare fractions.

Examples:

$\frac{1}{2} = \frac{3}{6} : \frac{1}{2}$ is equivalent to $\frac{3}{6}$

$\frac{2}{4} < \frac{3}{5} : \frac{2}{4}$ is less than $\frac{3}{5}$

$\frac{2}{3} > \frac{1}{4} : \frac{2}{3}$ is greater than $\frac{1}{4}$

$\frac{1}{8} < \frac{2}{5} < \frac{6}{7} : \frac{2}{5}$ is between $\frac{1}{8}$ and $\frac{6}{7}$

You can compare two fractions by *cross multiplying*: multiplying the numerator of each fraction with the denominator of the other. The greater cross product indicates the greater fraction:

Compare $\frac{11}{13}$ and $\frac{7}{8}$ by cross multiplying.

$$\frac{11}{13} \times \frac{7}{8}$$

$8 \times 11 = 88$ $7 \times 13 = 91$

$88 < 91$, so $\frac{11}{13} < \frac{7}{8}$

Computing with Fractions

Adding and subtracting fractions:

To add and subtract fractions, write the fractions so that they have a common denominator. Then add or subtract the numerators and then write the answer as a fraction in the simplest form (often a mixed number).

Example: Add:

$$\frac{2}{3} + \frac{3}{4} ; \frac{2}{3} = \frac{8}{12} ; \frac{3}{4} = \frac{9}{12} ; \frac{8}{12} + \frac{9}{12} = \frac{17}{12} = 1\frac{5}{12}$$

Example: Subtract:

$$\frac{5}{6} - \frac{1}{3} ; \frac{5}{6} = \frac{5}{6} ; \frac{1}{3} = \frac{2}{6} ; \frac{5}{6} - \frac{2}{6} = \frac{3}{6} = \frac{1}{2}$$

Multiplying fractions:

To multiply fractions, first change any mixed numbers into improper fractions. Multiply the numerators and multiply the denominators. Then write the answer in the simplest form.

Example: Multiply:

$$2\frac{1}{4} \times \frac{2}{3} \; ; \; \frac{9}{4} \times \frac{2}{3} = \frac{18}{12} = 1\frac{6}{12} = 1\frac{1}{2}$$

Dividing fractions:

To divide fractions, first change any mixed numbers into improper fractions. Invert the divisor and then multiply. Then write the answer in the simplest form.

Example: Divide:

$$3\frac{2}{5} \div \frac{1}{4} \; ; \; \frac{17}{5} \div \frac{1}{4} \; ; \; \frac{17}{5} \times \frac{4}{1} = \frac{68}{5} = 13\frac{3}{5}$$

Percent

A percent is an amount per hundred. For example, 30% indicates 30 out of 100, which is equivalent to $\frac{30}{100}$ or $30 \div 100$.

Decimals can be written as percents and vice versa. To represent a decimal as a percent, move the decimal point two places to the right and add the percent sign.

Examples: 0.45 = 45%; 0.375 = 37.5%.

To represent percents as decimals, move the decimal point two places to the left and remove the percent sign.

Examples: 28% = 0.28; 87.4% = 0.874.

Fractions can also be written as percents and vice versa.

To represent a fraction as a percent, divide the numerator by the denominator. Write the resulting decimal as a percent.

Example:

$$\frac{3}{4} = 4\overline{)3.00}^{\;.75} = 75\%$$

Alternatively, to represent a fraction as a percent, write an equivalent fraction with 100 as the denominator. Write the numerator as a percent.

Example:

$$\frac{2}{5} = \frac{40}{100} = 40\%$$

To represent a percent as a fraction, write the number in the percent as the numerator and 100 as the denominator and simplify.

Example:

$$25\% = \frac{25}{100} = \frac{1}{4}$$

To find the percent of a number, multiply the number by the decimal representation of the percent.

Example: Find 25% of 300

$$0.25 \times 300 = 75.00 = 75$$

You can also find the percent of a number by multiplying the number by the fractional representation of the percent.

Example: Find 20% of 225.

$$20\% = \frac{20}{100} = \frac{1}{5} \; ; \; \frac{1}{5} \times 225 = \frac{225}{5} = 45$$

Estimation

Estimation skills are often used to plan daily activities. You might estimate the time it takes to run errands in order to plan out your day. You might estimate the cost of an upcoming vacation in order to begin saving enough money. On the *ParaPro Assessment,* estimation will be useful in two ways. First, you will encounter questions that may ask you to estimate the result of a problem. Second, estimation can help you confirm that you have chosen the correct answer for a computation problem.

Estimation often involves *rounding* to the nearest 10, 100, 1,000, etc. If the number is *less than half* of the value of the place you are rounding to, round *down*. If the number is *greater than* or *equal to* half of the value of the place you are rounding to, round *up*.

Example: Rounding to the nearest 100: if the last two digits are less than 50, round down; if the last two digits are greater than or equal to 50, round up.

Rounding 537 to the nearest 100: 37 is less than 50; estimated number is 500.

The questions on the *ParaPro Assessment,* will ask you to estimate the result of an addition, subtraction, multiplication, or division problem. To solve these problems, round the numbers to the place value that would simplify the calculation and provide the best estimate.

Example: Which of the following is closest to 78×824?

   (A) 56,000
   (B) 64,000
   (C) 70,000
   (D) 74,000

Rounding each number gives you the estimate $80 \times 800 = 64,000$. (The exact result is 64,272.)

Decimals can be estimated in a similar way. Round each decimal to the place value that would simplify the calculation and provide the best estimate.

Example: Which of the following is closest to 0.021×68?

   (A)   1.2
   (B)   1.4
   (C) 12
   (D) 14

Rounding each number would give you the estimate $0.02 \times 70 = 1.40$, or 1.4. (The exact result is 1.428.)

Word Problems

Below are some general strategies for approaching word problems:

- Determine precisely what information the question is asking for.

- Determine what operations (addition, subtraction, multiplication, division, etc.) will help you solve the problem. See the word list below to help you identify which operations may be appropriate.

- Determine what information can help you solve the problem. If you are taking the exam in paper form, you might want to circle the phrases that contain information essential to solving the problem.

- When appropriate, rewrite the question as a number sentence or equation. For example, if the word problem asks you to find what number added to 10 results in 25, you could write a number sentence as follows: $n + 10 = 25$.

Below is a list of words most commonly associated with each kind of operation.

Addition:

- sum: What is the sum of ....?

- plus: What is the result of n plus m?

Subtraction:

- difference: What is the difference of ...?

- less: How much less is n than m?

- decreased by: How much is n decreased by?

Multiplication:

- product: What is the product of n and m?

- times: What is n times m?

- of: What is $n\%$ of m?

Division:

- quotient: What is the quotient of ...?

- per: How many n per m?

Comparison:

- equals, is equal to: What fraction is equal to *n*?

- greater than (or equal to): Which is greater than or equal to *n*?

- less than (or equal to): Which is less than or equal to *n*?

Some word problems require you to apply math skills to real-life situations. The following is an example of this:

There are 28 families in a neighborhood. If 25% of the families have pets, how many families in the neighborhood have pets?

- A) 7
- B) 14
- C) 21
- D) 25

Answer

This word problem asks you to work with percent. First, identify what information the question is looking for. This question is asking for the number of families in the neighborhood that have pets, which can be determined by finding what number is 25% of 28. Convert the percent to a fraction: $25\% = \frac{1}{4}$. Then multiply the fraction by the total number of families: $\frac{1}{4} \times 28$. Alternately, you can convert 25% to the decimal 0.25 and multiply 28 by 0.25.

$$\frac{1}{4} \times 28 = 0.25 \times 28 = 7$$

Therefore, the correct answer is (A); 7 families in the neighborhood have pets.

Linear Equations

Linear equations are equations that help you solve for an unknown quantity. In equations, this unknown quantity is called a *variable* and is represented by a letter (for example, x).

The key to solving a linear equation is to isolate the variable on one side of the equation. Below are strategies for solving common linear equations:

Addition:

Isolate the variable by subtracting the same value from both sides.

Example:

$$x + 3 = 7$$
$$x + 3 - 3 = 7 - 3$$
$$x = 4$$

Subtraction:

Isolate the variable by adding the same value from both sides.

Example:

$$x - 2 = 4$$
$$x - 2 + 2 = 4 + 2$$
$$x = 6$$

Multiplication:

Isolate the variable by dividing both sides by the same value.

Example:

$$4x = 12$$
$$\frac{4x}{4} = \frac{12}{4}$$
$$x = 3$$

Division:

Isolate the variable by multiplying both sides by the same value.

Example:

$$x \div 7 = 3$$
$$\frac{x}{7} = 3$$
$$\frac{x}{7}(7) = 3(7)$$
$$x = 21$$

Using Linear Equations to Solve Word Problems

You have already used linear equations to solve problems.

For example: "What number added to 10 results in 25?" is rewritten as $n + 10 = 25$; so, $n = 15$.

 Expert tips:

Use the tips below to use equations to solve word problems:

- Locate the information that needs to be identified. That quantity will be represented by a variable (for example, x).

- Solve the equation by isolating the variable.

Example: What number multiplied by 3 results in 126?

Answer

Let x represent the number multiplied by 3 and rewrite the problem as the following linear equation:

$$3x = 126$$

To solve the equation, divide both sides by 3.

$$\frac{3x}{3} = \frac{126}{3}$$

$$x = 42$$

Therefore, 42 is the number that when multiplied by 3 equals 126

Sequences

A list of numbers that follows a specific pattern is called a sequence. For example, in the sequence: 8, 13, 18, 23, ... each term after the first is 5 more than the term before it. The three dots at the end of the list of numbers indicates that this sequence goes on forever.

Number sequence questions might ask for the value of a term that is not shown in the given sequence.

For example: In the sequence 7, 13, 25, 49, ... each term after the first is 1 less than 2 times the previous term. What is the 6th term in the sequence?

To determine the 6th term, first calculate the 5th term by doubling the 4th term and subtracting 1.

$$2(49) - 1 = 98 - 1 = 97$$

Then double the 5th term and subtract 1 to calculate the 6th term.

$$2(97) - 1 = 194 - 1 = 193$$

Thus, the 6th term is 193.

2 Geometry and Measurement

Identifying Geometric Shapes

Below is a list of common geometric shapes.

Polygon: a closed plane formed by three or more line segments. Polygons that have all sides and angles of equal measurement are called *regular polygons*.

Examples of polygons are shown below:

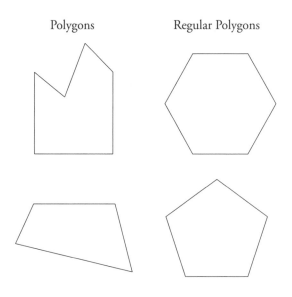

Polygons   Regular Polygons

Triangle: any three-sided polygon. Special triangles include

- Equilateral triangle: a triangle with all three sides the same length

- Isosceles triangle: a triangle with two sides having the same length

- Right triangle: a triangle containing a 90° angle

Examples of triangles are shown below:

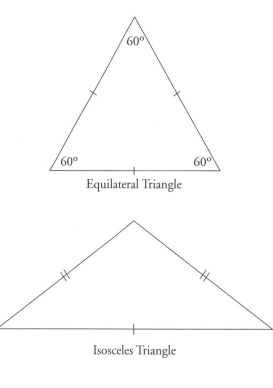

Equilateral Triangle

Isosceles Triangle

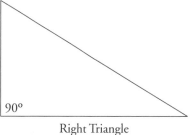

Right Triangle

Quadrilateral: any four-sided polygon. Special quadrilaterals include

- Rectangle: a quadrilateral with four right angles

- Square: a rectangle with all sides having the same length

Examples of quadrilaterals are shown below:

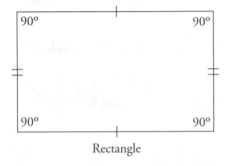

Rectangle

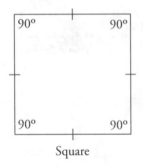

Square

Other polygons: You can often tell how many sides a polygon has by its name. Here are some other common polygons:

- Pentagon: a five-sided polygon

- Hexagon: a six-sided polygon

- Octagon: an eight-sided polygon

Examples of polygons are shown below:

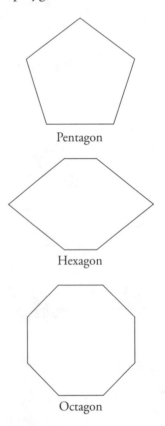

Pentagon

Hexagon

Octagon

Circle: A circle is a closed plane curve on which every point is equidistant from a center point. Important parts of a circle to know are

- Radius: a straight line that has an endpoint at the center of the circle and an endpoint on the circle

- Diameter: a straight line that passes through the center of a circle and has endpoints on the circle

- Circumference: the distance around the circle (the perimeter of the circle)

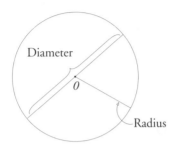

Three-dimensional figures: There are special names for certain three-dimensional figures:

- Rectangular solid: three-dimensional figure formed by six rectangular surfaces or faces

- Cube: a rectangular solid in which all edges are of equal length

Examples of three-dimensional figures are shown below:

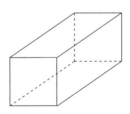

Rectangular Solid

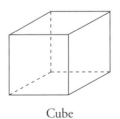

Cube

xy-Coordinate Planes

The coordinate plane has an *x*-axis and a *y*-axis that are perpendicular (intersect at a 90° angle). The *x*-axis is horizontal; the *y*-axis is vertical. Points are expressed as the coordinate pair (*x*, *y*). The intersection of the *x*-axis and the *y*-axis is called the *origin*. The *origin (0)* is the coordinate pair (0,0). On the *x*-axis, any *x* coordinate to the left of the *y*-axis is negative; any *x* coordinate to the right of the *y*-axis is positive. On the *y*-axis, any *y* coordinate below the *x*-axis is negative; any *y* coordinate above the *y*-axis is positive.

Plot coordinate pairs by beginning at the origin (0,0). Count the number to the left or right indicated by the *x* coordinate. From that position on the *x*-axis, count the number up or down indicated by the *y* coordinate. This final position locates the point.

Example: Plot the following coordinate pairs on the grid below:

A (3, 2); B (−2, 4); C (−1, −3); D (4,0)

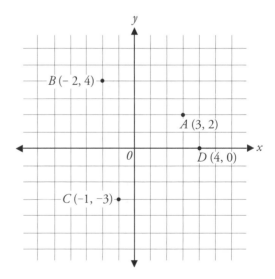

Units of Measurement

There are two systems of measurement in common use: the metric system and the customary English system. Below is a list of the most common units of measure in each system.

Metric system:

Length

Units: 1 meter = 1,000 millimeters
1 meter = 100 centimeters
1 kilometer = 1,000 meters

Weight

Units: 1 gram = 1,000 milligrams
1 kilogram = 1,000 grams

Capacity

Units: 1 liter = 1,000 milliliters
1 kiloliter = 1,000 liters

Customary English system:

Length

Units: 1 foot = 12 inches
1 yard = 3 feet = 36 inches
1 mile =1,760 yards = 5,280 feet

Weight

Units: 1 pound = 16 ounces

Capacity

Units: 1 cup = 8 fluid ounces
1 pint = 2 cups
1 quart = 2 pints
1 gallon = 4 quarts

Conversions

You may be asked to convert between different units within the same measurement system.

To convert larger units into smaller units, multiply by the number of parts per whole.

To convert smaller units into larger units, divide by the number of parts per whole.

Metric system

Example: How many meters are there in 432 centimeters?

Solution: A meter is equal to 100 centimeters. To convert centimeters to meters, divide the number of centimeters by 100.

$$\frac{432 \text{ cm}}{100} = 4.32 \text{ meters}$$

Example: How many liters are there in 0.05 kiloliter?

Solution: A kiloliter is equal to 1,000 liters. To convert kiloliters to liters, multiply the number of kiloliters by 1,000.

$$0.05 \text{ kl} \times 1,000 = 50 \text{ liters}$$

Customary English system

Example: How many quarts are there in 4 gallons?

Solution: 1 gallon = 4 quarts (4 parts per whole)

To find the number of quarts, multiply by 4.

$$4 \text{ gallons} \times 4 = 16 \text{ quarts}$$

Example: How many yards are there in 21 feet?

Solution: 1 yard = 3 feet (3 parts per whole)

To find the number of yards, divide the number of feet by 3.

$$21 \text{ feet} \div 3 = 7 \text{ yards}$$

Perimeter, Area, and Volume

Perimeter

Perimeter is the sum of the lengths of all of the sides of a polygon or the length of the complete arc that defines a circle.

To calculate the perimeter of a polygon, add the length of each side. The total will be the perimeter.

Example: A rectangle has a length of 5 and a width of 3. What is its perimeter?

Solution: 5 + 5 + 3 + 3 = 16

The perimeter of a circle has a special name—the circumference. The circumference of a circle can be calculated by multiplying the radius (r) by 2π:

$$C = 2\pi r$$

Example: A circle has a radius of 4. What is its circumference?

Solution: $2 \times \pi \times 4 = 8\pi$

Area

Area is the amount of space enclosed by a polygon or circle. Below is a list of formulas for the areas of the most common geometric shapes.

Triangle:

$$\text{Area} = \frac{1}{2}\text{base} \times \text{height} = \frac{1}{2}bh$$

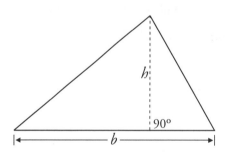

Rectangle: Area = length × width = lw

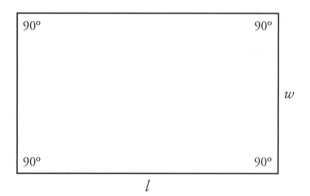

Square: Area = (length of a side)² = s^2

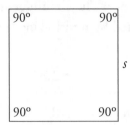

Circle: Area = radius² × π = πr^2

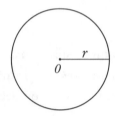

Volume

Volume is the amount of space enclosed by a three-dimensional figure. The formulas for the volumes of a rectangular solid and a cube are given below.

Rectangular solid: Volume = length × width × height = (*lwh*)

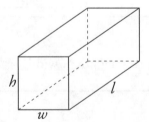

Cube: Volume = (length of a side)³ = $(s)^3$

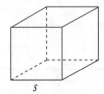

Time

Below are common units of time:

Units: 1 minute = 60 seconds
       1 hour = 60 minutes
       1 day = 24 hours

You may be asked to convert among units of time. Units of time are related to each other as parts of wholes.

- To convert larger units into smaller units, multiply by the number of parts per whole.

- To convert smaller units into larger units, divide by the number of parts per whole.

Example: How many minutes are there in 3 hours?

Solution: 1 hour = 60 minutes (60 parts per whole)

To find the number of minutes, multiply by 60.

$$3 \text{ hours} \times 60 = 180 \text{ minutes}$$

Example: How many minutes are there in 7,680 seconds?

Solution: 1 minute = 60 seconds (60 parts per whole)

To find the number of minutes, divide by 60.

$$7,680 \text{ seconds} \div 60 = 128 \text{ minutes}$$

You also may be asked to convert between different ways of expressing time. Here are the common ways of expressing time.

Numerical expressions represent the time by providing the numerical hour and then minutes, separated by a colon and followed by A.M. or P.M. (e.g., 1:30 P.M.). The most common expressions of time rely on a 12-hour cycle; two 12-hour cycles = 1 day.

Verbal expressions represent time by indicating the hour and the minutes in relation to the hour. Verbal expressions use the term *o'clock* to indicate the hour and the terms *quarter past, half past,* and *quarter to* in order to indicate fifteen-minute intervals.

Numerical expression:	*Verbal expression:*
5:00 P.M.	Five o'clock in the evening
4:15 A.M.	A quarter past four in the morning
2:30 P.M.	Half-past two in the afternoon
7:45 A.M.	A quarter to eight in the morning
12:00 P.M.	Noon; twelve o'clock in the afternoon
12:00 A.M.	Midnight; twelve o'clock in the morning

Money

Below are the basic units for money in the United States.

Basic unit: 1 cent = 0.01 dollar ($0.01)

Other units:
1 nickel = 5 cents
1 dime = 10 cents
1 quarter = 25 cents
1 half-dollar = 50 cents
1 dollar = 100 cents

You can represent money either as a word phrase (1 nickel, 5 cents) or using the dollar sign and decimal (four dollars and twenty-five cents = $4.25).

You may be asked to help students convert between different denominations (units of money). Use the following techniques to help you in the conversion.

To convert from larger to smaller denominations:

■ Write the amount in dollar-sign form.

■ Multiply by 100 to convert to cents.

■ Then divide by the number of cents for the unit of measure you are converting to.

Example: How many dimes are there in 3 dollars?

Solution: $3 × 100 = 300 cents
300 cents ÷ 10 = 30 dimes

To convert from smaller to larger denominations:

■ Write the amount as cents.

■ Multiply by the original unit (cents/denomination).

■ Divide by the new unit (cents/denomination).

Example: How many quarters are there in 50 nickels?

Solution: 50 nickels × 5 = 250 cents
250 cents ÷ 25 = 10 quarters

3 Data Organization and Interpretation

Graphs

Graphs are ways of visually representing comparisons between amounts or shifts over time. Four different types of graphs are illustrated and explained below:

Bar graphs

Bar graphs are generally used to compare amounts; the longer the bar, the greater the amount. To read bar graphs, follow the procedure used in the example below:

Find how many students graduated from Dalton County High School in 1998.

NUMBER OF GRADUATING STUDENTS IN DALTON COUNTY HIGH SCHOOL

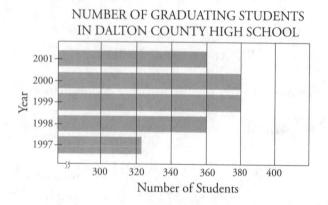

- Identify the bar that represents the information you need; in this case, the date 1998 on the vertical axis.

- Follow the bar to its end; from that point, drop down in a straight line to the numbers on the horizontal axis. That number is your answer. In this example, the answer is 360 students.

Line graphs

Line graphs are generally used to illustrate trends, often over time. To read line graphs, follow the procedure used in the example below:

Find the total number of motors produced in September by National Motors.

NUMBER OF MOTORS PRODUCED BY NATIONAL MOTORS

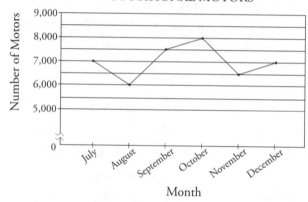

- In this case, the solid line represents the number of motors produced by National Motors.

- Find the specific information you need on the axis that represents that information. For example, on the horizontal "Month" axis, locate September.

- Move up to the line. From that point, move over to the vertical axis to read the amount. For this example, the number of motors produced in September by National Motors is 7,500.

Pictographs

Pictographs compare amounts by using symbols to stand for numbers; the greater the number of symbols, the greater the amount. Often the symbols will represent a specific number of units; for example, 1 symbol could represent 1,000 units. Sometimes only half of a symbol will be drawn; this means that it represents only half of the total number of units that the whole symbol represents. To read pictographs, follow the procedure used in the example below:

Find the number of plates sold in Fielding's Department Store for February.

NUMBER OF PLATES SOLD
IN FOUR STORES IN FEBRUARY

Wilson's Kitchen Outlets	○ ○ ○
Kitchen Junction	○ ○ ○ ○ ◖
Fielding's Department Store	○ ○ ○ ○
Karen's Crystal	○ ○ ○

Each ○ represents 100 plates.

- Identify the set of symbols that represents the information you need, in this case, the symbols that represent the number of plates sold in Fielding's Department Store.

- Count the number of symbols and multiply that number by the number they represent; the solution for this problem is

$$4 \bigcirc \times 100 = 400 \text{ plates.}$$

Circle graphs

Circle graphs (also known as pie charts) visually compare percent of a whole. The "slices" (or sectors) of a circle graph represent the percents of the total. To read circle graphs, follow the procedure used in the example below:

PERCENT OF COMPETITORS
IN THE CITY TRIATHLON BY AGE

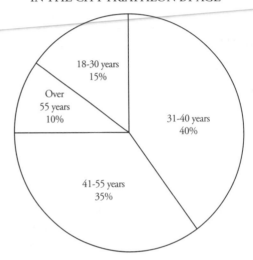

A total of 320 competitors participated in this year's City Triathlon. How many of the participants were over 55 years old?

- Identify the percent of competitors who were over 55 years old. According to the graph, 10% of the participants were over 55 years old.

- Set up a simple equation using the percent represented by the "slice" and the total number that the whole circle represents.

10% of 320 = 0.1 × 320 = 32. The number of participants over the age of 55 was 32.

Tables

Tables are another means of representing data in a comparative way. Tables can be used to represent comparative amounts within a total or percent of the total. To gather information and solve problems using a table, follow the procedure used in the example below:

FREQUENCY OF PET
OWNERSHIP IN UNIONVILLE

Number of Pets Owned	Percent of Unionville Households
0	32%
1	41%
2	18%
3 or more	9%

Example: What percent of Unionville households own 2 or more pets?

Solution: Add the percents for both "2" and "3 or more": 18% + 9% = 27%

Trends

The values on a graph follow a trend if at certain time intervals these values follow a specific pattern. For instance, in the graph below, for every year starting with 1999, the number of nursing degrees awarded has been 4 more than the previous year.

NURSING DEGREES AWARDED,
1998-2001

A question on this test might ask you to determine the number of nursing degrees awarded in 2004 if this trend continues. To answer this question, determine the pattern or trend, number of nursing degrees awarded in the last year shown on the graph, and the number of years from 2001 to 2004. According to the graph, the number of nursing degrees awarded each year is 4 more than the previous year, and the number of nursing degrees awarded in 2001 is 44. Since the number of years from 2001 to 2004 is 3 and the number of nursing degrees awarded increases by 4 degrees each year, the increase in the number of degrees awarded in 2004 can be forecast by multiplying 3 years and 4 degrees per year.

$$3 \times 4 = 12$$

Therefore, the number of nursing degrees forecast to be awarded in 2004 is 44 + 12 = 56.

Mean, Median, Mode

You may be presented with a list of numbers and asked to calculate either the *mean*, the *median*, or the *mode*. Definitions of these terms are provided below.

Mean: The mean is the average of the numbers in the list. A mean is calculated by adding together all of the numbers in the list and then dividing the sum by the number of numbers in the list.

Example: For the numbers 2, 3, 7, 12, calculate the mean.

Add the numbers: 2 + 3 + 7 + 12 = 24

Divide the sum of the numbers by the number of numbers: 24 ÷ 4 = 6.

The mean is 6.

Median: The median is the middle number when a list of numbers are ordered from least to greatest. The median of a list with an even number of numbers is the average (arithmetic mean) of the two middle values, when the numbers in the list are ordered from least to greatest.

Example: For the numbers 1, 19, 19, 2, 15, find the median.

Place the numbers in order from least to greatest: 1, 2, 15, 19, 19

The median is the third, or middle, number: 15

Example: For the numbers 20, 8, 4, 16, find the median.

Place the numbers in order from least to greatest: 4, 8, 16, 20

Find the average (arithmetic mean) of the two middle numbers: $\frac{8 + 16}{2} = 12$.

The median is 12.

Mode: The mode is the number that appears most frequently in a list of numbers.

Example: For the numbers 3, 4, 8, 3, 8, 2, 8, find the mode.

Count the number of times each number appears: 2 and 4 appear one time each; 3 appears two times; 8 appears three times.

The mode is 8 because 8 appears most frequently.

General Test-Taking Tips for Math Skills Questions

- Use the examples in the review course as guides to help you identify the types of problems you will encounter on the test. Identifying question types can help you immediately focus your approach to the problem on a specific set of steps you can take to reach the solution.

- The first step to answering most problems is to identify the information that the question is looking for. By identifying the information needed, you focus immediately on the specific strategies you can use to answer the question.

- Be aware that not all questions require computation. Sometimes you will be able to identify the correct answer simply by looking at a graph or figure.

- When you do encounter problems that may require a short series of computations, make sure that you work through each required step to find the precise information required. Don't stop before a complete result is found.

Part II. Application of Math Skills and Knowledge to Classroom Instruction

Mathematics Application questions are typically based on classroom scenarios in which students are involved in math-related tasks that draw upon the categories of math concepts listed in the Math Skills and Knowledge Section. These questions focus on testing mathematical competencies needed to assist the teacher with instruction. The test questions do not require knowledge of advanced-level mathematics vocabulary. You may not use calculators.

While these questions draw upon the math skills and knowledge that you used in the first part of this chapter, these questions will be oriented to two different contexts. These two contexts are discussed below.

The General School or Classroom Context

Some questions will reflect the kind of math skills necessary for facilitating general school or classroom duties that a paraprofessional may encounter, such as scheduling time for class activities, organizing students into groups, managing classroom materials, and so on. Below are some expert tips to keep in mind as you encounter this kind of question.

Expert tips:

- These questions ask you to apply your math skills to actual school and classroom situations. You will have to solve a problem completely using your math skills.

- Many of these questions will be in the form of word problems. Review the approaches to word problems in the Math Skills and Knowledge section.

The following is an example of a question that requires you to apply math skills within a classroom context.

AFTERNOON CLASS SCHEDULE

Activity	Time (hours)
Lunch	$\dfrac{3}{4}$
Language arts	$1\dfrac{1}{4}$
Science	$\dfrac{1}{2}$
Computer	$\dfrac{1}{3}$

According to the class schedule above, how many hours are spent each afternoon on language arts, science, and computer activities?

(A) $1\dfrac{3}{9}$

(B) $1\dfrac{3}{4}$

(C) 2

(D) $2\dfrac{1}{12}$

This question asks you to apply your word problem, table-reading, and fraction skills for a professional purpose. First, identify what the question is asking for; it is asking for a sum total of the hours spent each afternoon on language arts, science, and computer activities. Then read the chart to identify the amounts of time spent on each activity: $1\dfrac{1}{4}$, $\dfrac{1}{2}$, and $\dfrac{1}{3}$ hours, respectively. To add these fractions, you must change them to fractions with a common denominator. For this question, the common denominator is 12.

$$1\dfrac{1}{4}+\dfrac{1}{2}+\dfrac{1}{3}=\dfrac{5}{4}+\dfrac{1}{2}+\dfrac{1}{3}=$$

$$\dfrac{15}{12}+\dfrac{6}{12}+\dfrac{4}{12}=\dfrac{25}{12}=2\dfrac{1}{12}$$

The correct answer is (D).

The Instructional Context

Others questions will ask you to help instruct students in specific, math-related tasks in the classroom. You may be helping students learn new vocabulary or work through the individual steps to solve a problem, or you may be confirming that a student's answer is correct. Below are some expert tips to keep in mind as you encounter this kind of question.

Expert tips:

- These questions may ask you to assist students with either word problems or number problems. Be prepared to encounter either form.

- Distinguish between questions that ask you to work with a *step* in solving a problem and questions that ask you to *solve* a problem. Sometimes instructional context questions ask you to identify and/or correct a preliminary step necessary for the student to take in order to solve the problem. You may not have to solve the student's math problem in order to answer the question.

- It may help you to review the math skills and knowledge covered in this chapter, with an emphasis on the steps necessary to solve each kind of problem. This knowledge will be helpful in an instructional context.

The following is an example of a question that requires an application of math skills within an instructional context.

$$4 + 5 \times 6 + 3 = ?$$

A student wrote the incorrect number sentence above to solve the following problem:

"Multiply the sum of 4 and 5 and the sum of 6 and 3."

To correct the error, the student's number sentence should be changed to

(A) $4 + (5 \times 6) + 3 = ?$
(B) $(4 + 5 \times 6 + 3) = ?$
(C) $(4 + 5) \times (6 + 3) = ?$
(D) $(4 + 5 \times 6) + 3 = ?$

Answer

This question asks you to correctly identify and represent the order of operations. The question asks the student to calculate the sums *before* multiplying. This means that the sums must be represented in parentheses. The correct answer is (C), $(4 + 5) \times (6 + 3) = ?$.

Let's Try It!

Sample Questions

Now try to answer the sample questions below. Keep track of the questions that you miss; then go back to the review course and examine the appropriate sections. Remember to focus on the steps in the process, not just on the correct answer.

1. 672 ÷ 14 =

   (A) 40

   (B) 48

   (C) $\frac{1}{48}$

   (D) $\frac{1}{14}$

Answer

This computation question requires long-division skills. Rewrite the problem as below:

$$
\begin{array}{r}
48 \\
14\overline{)672} \\
-56 \\
\hline
112 \\
-112 \\
\hline
0
\end{array}
$$

The correct answer is (B), 48.

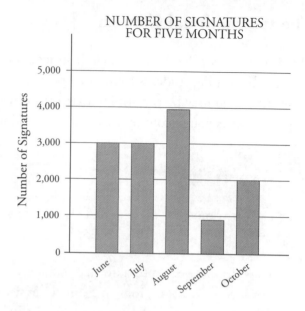

NUMBER OF SIGNATURES
FOR FIVE MONTHS

2. According to the graph above, the total number of signatures obtained for the five months shown is

   (A) less than 11,000
   (B) between 11,000 and 12,000
   (C) between 12,000 and 13,000
   (D) greater than 13,000

Answer

This question asks you to interpret data from a graph. First, find the information being sought in the word problem; the question asks you to find the total number of signatures for all five months and compare the total to the answers provided. To find the total number of signatures, you must identify how many signatures were found each month and then add the results.

Add: 3,000 + 3,000 + 3,900 + 800 + 2,000 = 12,700. Then compare the result to the answers provided. Since 12,000 < 12,700 < 13,000, only answer (C), *between* 12,000 and 13,000, is correct.

3. What is the approximate value of $\frac{9,850}{248.2}$?

   (A)   4
   (B)   40
   (C)   400
   (D) 4,000

Answer

This question requires estimation. Round each number and then divide. Round 9,850 to 10,000 and 248.2 to 250.

$$\frac{10,000}{250} = 40$$

Therefore, the correct answer is (B), 40.

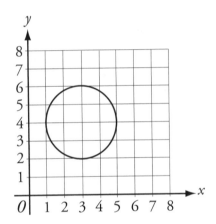

4. Which of the following points is in the circle in the *xy*-plane shown above?

   (A) (3, 5)
   (B) (4, 7)
   (C) (5, 1)
   (D) (6, 3)

This question asks you to identify a point on an *xy*-coordinate plane. First, graph each of the points in options (A), (B), (C), and (D) as shown below.

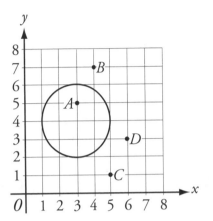

As can be seen on the graph, *A* (3,5) is in the circle.

5. The senior class wants to carpet the school entrance as a class gift. The carpet costs $3 per square foot. If the entrance is rectangular with a length of 12 feet and a width of 10 feet, what is the cost, in dollars, of the carpet?

   (A) $66
   (B) $300
   (C) $360
   (D) $442

Answer

This question is a word problem. First, identify what the question is asking for. In this example, the question is asking you to calculate the cost of carpeting a rectangular school entrance. So, you must find the area of the entrance and then multiply that by the cost per square foot in order to find the final cost.

Find the area of the school entrance, using the formula for a rectangle (length multiplied by width):

$$12 \text{ feet} \times 10 \text{ feet} = 120 \text{ square feet}$$

Then multiply the result by the cost per square foot:

$$120 \text{ square feet} \times \$3 = \$360$$

The correct answer is (C), $360.

6. Which of the following is less than 0.032?

    (A)   0.22
    (B)   0.1
    (C)   0.0297
    (D)   0.31

This question asks you to order numbers according to place value.

First, compare the value of each digit in the tenths place.

$$0.22 > 0.032$$
$$0.1 > 0.032$$
$$0.31 > 0.032$$

This comparison shows that the numbers 0.0297 and 0.032 both have the digit 0 in the tenths place. In this case, compare the values of the digits in the hundredths place.

The value of the digit in the hundredths place of 0.0297 is less than the value of the digit in the hundredths place of 0.032: (i.e., 2 < 3). Therefore, the correct answer is (C), 0.0297 < 0.032.

7. If $\frac{x}{4} = 12$, what is the value of x?

    (A) $\frac{1}{3}$
    (B) 3
    (C) 24
    (D) 48

Answer

This question asks you to solve a linear equation. Recall that to solve a linear equation, you must isolate the variable (x) on one side of the equal sign. Since the variable is divided by 4, to isolate the variable you must multiply both sides by 4.

$$\frac{x}{4}(4) = 12(4)$$

Since $12 \times 4 = 48$, the correct answer is (D).

Chapter 6

Writing Review Course with Sample Questions

▶ ▶ ▶ ▶ ▶ ▶ ▶ ▶ ▶ ▶ ▶ ▶

Overview

The 30 questions in the writing section of the *ParaPro Assessment* fall into two categories:

I. Writing Skills and Knowledge (approximately 18 questions)

II. Application of Writing Skills and Knowledge to Classroom Instruction (approximately 12 questions)

All questions are multiple-choice; you will not be required to do any writing. Instead, these questions focus on common elements of grammar, sentence structure, and the writing process.

The first category of questions tests your ability to recognize and appropriately use knowledge and skills for building sentences. This includes identifying different parts of speech and different parts of sentences (e.g., nouns, adjectives, subjects, predicates), recognizing basic grammar mistakes, and identifying incorrect spellings of common words.

The second category of questions tests your ability to *apply* your writing skills and knowledge to classroom instruction. These questions draw on many of the sentence-building skills described above. In addition, the Writing Application questions ask you to apply your knowledge of common writing activities such as outlining, developing main ideas for paragraphs, and revising sentences for clarity and correctness. These questions probably look slightly different from questions you may have seen on other tests because they present an actual classroom situation or activity, but to answer them you need only apply your writing knowledge and skills. You do *not* need special knowledge of writing pedagogy (philosophies or approaches to teaching writing) to answer the questions, though you will probably draw on your own experiences of drafting and revising written work.

Some common rules of grammar, punctuation, and word usage are discussed in the review course that begins on the next page, followed by sample questions. If you would like additional help, look through an up-to-date writing handbook. There are many different styles of writing handbooks, so you should spend some time locating the one that feels most comfortable to you.

Part I: The Writing Skills and Knowledge Section

What's Being Tested?

The Writing Skills and Knowledge questions measure your ability to recognize elements of sentences as well as many common grammar, word usage, and spelling mistakes. Your ability to answer these questions will be based on your knowledge of how to create clear, correct sentences.

In the Writing Skills and Knowledge questions you may be asked to identify

- basic grammatical errors in standard written English

- errors in word usage (e.g., their/they're/there, then/than)

- errors in punctuation

- parts of speech (nouns, verbs, pronouns, adjectives, adverbs, and prepositions)

- parts of a sentence (e.g., subject and verb/predicate)

- errors in spelling

REVIEW COURSE: Writing Skills and Knowledge

This review course covers many of the common elements of grammar and sentence construction that you need to know to do well on this test. The review course may use some grammar terms that are new to you. You do not need to know all of these terms to do well on the *ParaPro Assessment*. These terms are mentioned in case you want to consult a grammar handbook for more help. It is often easier to find out information about a particular grammar concept if you know what it is usually called in a grammar book.

If you come across terms in the review course that you do not understand, refer to the glossary on page 123.

Parts of Speech

Every word in a sentence can be classified as a part of speech. There are eight parts of speech:

- Noun

- Verb

- Adjective

- Adverb

- Pronoun

- Preposition

- Conjunction

- Interjection

In the *ParaPro Assessment*, you will need to know how to identify the first six parts of speech on this list (you will not need to know how to identify conjunctions or interjections). However, it is helpful to recognize conjunctions and interjections because they often serve as signals for particular kinds of punctuation.

Let's review the parts of speech and how to recognize them.

Noun

A **noun** is a word that names a person, place, thing, or concept.

Examples of nouns include *nurse* (person), *office* (place), *book* (thing), *happiness* (concept).

A **proper noun** is a noun that gives the name of a specific person, place, thing, or concept; it is always capitalized. Examples of proper nouns include *Ellen* (person), the *Grand Canyon* (place), the *Washington Monument* (thing), *Surrealism* (concept).

Verb

A **verb** is a word that tells what a subject does or is.

Examples of verbs include *walk, feel, led, is running, had eaten*. The base form of a verb is the phrase "*to* + verb": *to show, to fall, to seek, to read*. From this base form, the verb can change its form for one of several purposes. These include the following:

A verb can show time through its tense.

Example: to learn

Present tense: Tammy learns.
Past tense: Tammy learned.
Future tense: Tammy will learn.

A verb can indicate the number of the noun engaging in the action (singular—one; or plural—more than one).

Example: to sprint

Singular: The runner sprints to the finish line.
Plural: The runners sprint to the finish line.

Adjective

An **adjective** is a word that describes a noun or pronoun. Adjectives are said to *modify* nouns and pronouns because they help change a reader's understanding of a noun. Notice how your image of the dog changes in the following sentences:

Examples:

A <u>tired</u> dog sat on the porch next to the door.

An <u>angry</u> dog sat on the porch next to the door.

A <u>happy</u> dog sat on the porch next to the door.

Adverb

An **adverb** is a word that modifies a verb, an adjective, another adverb, or a clause. Adverbs are used to add detail and specificity to the action of a sentence.

Examples:

The adverb modifies a verb:

> Dan finished his dessert <u>quickly</u>.

The adverb modifies an adjective:

> The puzzle left him <u>completely</u> confused.

The adverb modifies another adverb:

> The cat climbed the tree <u>very</u> quickly.

The adverb modifies a clause:

> <u>Suddenly</u>, the lights went out.

Most adverbs end in *-ly*. They are often formed by adding *-ly* to adjectives.

Pronoun

A **pronoun** is a word that stands in for or refers to a noun. A pronoun can be personal (stands in for a noun) or possessive (refers to a noun).

Examples:

<u>He</u> baked a cake. (The pronoun *he* stands in for a noun, so it is a personal pronoun.)

Leticia fixed <u>her</u> car. (The pronoun *her* shows Leticia's possession of her car, so it is a possessive pronoun.)

Personal pronouns usually change their form depending on whether they are used as the subject (the person or thing performing the action) or object (the person or thing receiving the action) of a sentence.

Personal pronouns to use as subjects:
I, we, you, he, she, it, they

Personal pronouns to use as objects:
me, us, you, him, her, it, them

Examples:

<u>He</u> fell out of the boat. (*He* is the subject of the sentence.)

Alice gave the extra ticket to <u>me</u>. (*Me* is an object of the sentence.)

Possessive pronouns usually change form depending on whether they are used as adjectives or stand alone.

Possessive pronouns to use as adjectives:
my, our, your, his, her, its, their

Possessive pronouns to use standing alone:
mine, ours, yours, his, hers, its (rarely used), *theirs*

Examples:

<u>Her</u> book won the Pulitzer Prize. (*Her* modifies *book* and thus acts as an adjective.)

Alice took my sandwich and gave me <u>hers</u>. (*Hers* stands alone; it is an object of the sentence and is being used in place of the phrase *her sandwich*.)

Pronouns must agree in number with the noun for which they are standing in or to which they are referring. If a pronoun is used to stand in for *the students*, it should be a plural pronoun because it is referring to more than one student. The pronoun *they* is a plural pronoun and should be used in this case.

Pronouns must also agree in gender with the noun for which they are standing in or to which they refer. If a pronoun is used to stand in for the male name *Mark*, it should be a masculine pronoun, *he*.

Preposition

A **preposition** is a word used most often in front of a noun or pronoun that identifies a relationship such as time or space. Prepositions help provide more detail about an action.

Examples:

Portia drove <u>to</u> the bank. (The preposition *to* helps to show *where* Portia was driving.)

Josh hasn't seen Ken <u>since</u> Friday. (The preposition *since* helps to indicate *when* Josh last saw Ken.)

Common prepositions include *about, at, before, for, in, like, of, on, to, with*. Consult a grammar handbook for a more detailed list of prepositions.

Conjunction

A **conjunction** is a word that joins together two parts of a sentence.

Examples:

Amy ran the marathon <u>and</u> finished in record time.

Tony was nervous <u>but</u> excited to be selected for the job.

Common conjunctions include *and, but, or, yet, so, since, because*, and *when*. Some conjunctions work in pairs, such as *if/then, either/or, both/and*, and *not only/but also*. Consult a grammar handbook for a more detailed list of conjunctions.

Interjection

An **interjection** is a word that expresses emotion. It is inserted into a sentence or stands alone. Interjections usually are punctuated by exclamation points.

Examples:

<u>Wow!</u> Dante received an A on his research paper.

Trina lost control of her sled—<u>look out!</u>

Examples of interjections include: *wow!, oh my!, ha!,* and *neat!*

Parts of Sentences: Subject and Predicate

Every sentence has to have two essential parts in order to be a complete sentence: a **subject** (a person, place, or thing that is performing an action) and a **predicate** (the action that the subject performs or an assertion about that subject).

For example, in the sentence

Raoul has been working in his garden.

Raoul is the **subject** of the sentence. Raoul is performing an action (he *has been working* in his garden).

...*has been working in his garden* is the **complete predicate**. It characterizes Raoul. As a complete predicate, it includes both the main verb (*has been working*) and the person or thing receiving the action of the verb (*in his garden*).

...*has been working*... is the **simple predicate**. It consists only of the main verb in the sentence.

The subject of a sentence can be a common noun (*book, table, lamp*), a proper noun (*Reggie, Janet, the Secretary of Education*), or a pronoun (*I, you, they*); it may consist of a word, phrase, clause, or combination of nouns (*Tyrone and Laura, the first person who comes in the room, the woman wearing the baseball cap*). The simple predicate is always the main verb. The **complete predicate** includes the simple predicate but may also include adverbs, adjectives, prepositions, and prepositional phrases.

Grammar

Grammar is a system of rules that governs how words are used to form sentences. Grammar can be intimidating because it is often discussed using a highly specialized vocabulary; however, you do not need to know all of the grammar rules and vocabulary to identify and correct grammar mistakes effectively. Here are some of the aspects of grammar that are most important for students who are learning how to write and speak effectively.

Subject-verb agreement

Subjects and verbs have to indicate the same number; if a noun consists of a single thing, then the verb that goes with the noun must also be in a singular form. A sentence has a **subject-verb agreement error** when one word in a subject-verb pair is singular and the other word is plural.

Incorrect:

Birds flies.

This sentence is incorrect because the subject, *Birds,* is in a plural form while the verb, *flies,* is in a singular form.

You can correct sentences by changing the form of one of the words to make both words singular or both words plural.

Correct:

Birds fly.
(Both the subject and the verb are plural.)

A bird flies.
(Both the subject and the verb are singular.)

Verb tense

Each verb in a sentence must be in the proper tense. If two or more actions in a sentence occur at the same time, the verbs that indicate those actions must be in the same tense (for example, past tense or present tense). A sentence has a **verb tense error** if a verb in the sentence is in the wrong tense. Keeping all of the verbs in the same tense clarifies when the action in a sentence is taking place.

Incorrect:

During the committee meeting last week, Jessie <u>suggested</u> going to the beach, while Tracy <u>votes</u> for going to a museum.

(Both underlined verbs should be in the past tense because the phrase *During the committee meeting last week* indicates that both actions occurred in the past.)

You can correct the sentence by changing *votes* to past tense.

Correct:

During the committee meeting last week, Jessie <u>suggested</u> going to the beach, while Tracy <u>voted</u> for going to a museum.

(Both verbs are now in the past tense. Verbs in the past tense often end in *-ed.*)

Parallelism

When a sentence contains a series of items, all the items should be in parallel form. Keeping all phrases and clauses in the same form creates **parallelism** by clarifying the relationship among the parts of the sentence.

Incorrect:

Nadia enjoys <u>traveling</u> and <u>to visit</u> friends.

(This sentence is not parallel because *traveling* and *to visit* are not in the same form.)

You can correct sentences by putting both words in the same form.

Correct:

Nadia enjoys <u>traveling</u> and <u>visiting</u> friends.

(Both words are now in an *-ing* form.)

Noun-pronoun agreement

All pronouns and the nouns to which they refer must have the same number; both words must be singular or both words must be plural. If both words do not refer to the same number, the sentence has a **noun-pronoun agreement** error.

Incorrect:

I tried to go to <u>the supermarket</u> near my house, but <u>they</u> were closed.

(The sentence is incorrect because the noun, *supermarket,* is singular, and the pronoun, *they,* is plural.)

You can correct the sentence by making the pronoun singular.

Correct:

I tried to go to the <u>supermarket</u> near my house, but <u>it</u> was closed.

(Both noun and pronoun are singular. Note that the verb, *were,* also had to become singular to agree with the pronoun.)

Punctuation

Punctuation separates the different parts of a sentence and distinguishes between sentences. While there are many rules for punctuation, we will concentrate on three of the most common punctuation errors: comma usage, semicolon usage, and using apostrophes to show possession.

Comma usage

Commas are used to separate elements of a sentence. For example, they may be used to separate a series of words in a list or two separate clauses. A **clause** is a group of words that contains both a subject and a verb. Below are the four most common ways to use commas.

1. Use commas between two independent clauses that are connected by a **conjunction** such as *and, but, yet, or, nor, so,* or *for.* An **independent clause** is a clause with a subject and verb that does not depend upon another part of the sentence to clarify its meaning; it can stand alone as a complete sentence.

    Incorrect:

    Gemma won the election for student body president but Dana has more experience in leadership roles.

    Correct:

    Gemma won the election for student body president, but Dana has more experience in leadership roles.

    The sentence above should have a comma because it contains two independent clauses connected by the word *but* (a coordinating conjunction). You can tell that it has two independent clauses because each clause has a subject paired with its own verb: the independent clause *Gemma won the election for student body president* has a subject *(Gemma)* paired with a verb *(won),* and the independent clause *Dana has more experience in leadership roles* also has a subject *(Dana)* paired with a verb *(has).*

    A good test to determine whether a sentence requires a comma is to break it into two sentences where you think the comma might need to go (before the coordinating conjunction). If you end up with two complete sentences *(Gemma won the election for student body president. Dana has more experience in leadership roles.)* then you need a comma. Make sure you don't forget about the coordinating conjunction; a sentence of this type that has a comma but no coordinating conjunction is incorrect.

    Note: In very short sentences, the comma may be omitted, but it is not incorrect to put a comma as long as there are two independent clauses connected by a coordinating conjunction.

2. Use commas after an introductory element for a sentence that appears before the subject of the sentence.

    Incorrect:

    Before the race started Cliff stretched his muscles.

    Correct:

    Before the race started, Cliff stretched his muscles.

    Some writers do not use a comma after very short introductory elements. However, you should use a comma if the introductory element is long or if the comma would help clarify the meaning of the sentence.

3. Use commas before and after a clause or phrase that provides additional information that is not essential to the meaning of the sentence.

    Incorrect:

    My cousin an experienced pilot landed the plane safely.

    Correct:

    My cousin, an experienced pilot, landed the plane safely.

    Since the phrase *an experienced pilot* is not essential to understanding that the speaker's cousin landed the plane safely, it should be surrounded by commas.

4. Use commas to separate items in a series. When three or more items are used in a series, commas should separate the items.

    Incorrect:

    Seth has traveled to France Italy and the Czech Republic.

    Correct:

    Seth has traveled to France, Italy, and the Czech Republic.

    Some writers omit the comma before the last item in a series (before *and the Czech Republic*), but it is not incorrect to use a comma there.

Semicolon usage

Semicolons (;) are used to separate two independent clauses that are closely related in subject matter. (Remember, an **independent clause** is a clause with a subject and verb that does not depend on another part of the sentence to clarify its meaning; it can stand alone as a complete sentence.)

Incorrect:

Darrell wanted to wear his lucky tie for his job interview, unfortunately, the tie was at the cleaners.

Correct:

Darrell wanted to wear his lucky tie for his job interview; unfortunately, the tie was at the cleaners.

The sentence contains two complete independent clauses: *Darrell wanted to wear his lucky tie for his job interview*, and *unfortunately, the tie was at the cleaners*. You can tell that they are independent clauses because either clause could stand alone as a sentence. Therefore, they should be separated by a semicolon, not a comma.

Using apostrophes to show possession

Apostrophes (') can be used to show that a noun belongs to someone or something. Here are some common rules for using apostrophes.

Use apostrophes in the following situations:

1. To show possession for singular nouns: attach -'s

    Examples:

    the bird's wing, the host's party

2. To show possession for plural nouns that do not end in -s: attach -'s

    Examples:

    men's shoes, the mice's cheese

3. To show possession for plural nouns that end in -s: attach -'

    Examples:

    the dogs' howling, the players' rivalry

Do not use apostrophes in the following situations:

1. *Do not* use apostrophes for possessive pronouns:

    Example:

    Use *yours,* not *your's,* to show possession: *This coat must be yours.*

2. *Do not* use apostrophes to make nouns plural:

    Example:

    Use *ten fingers,* not *ten finger's*

Word Usage

Word usage refers to using words with meanings and forms that are appropriate for the context and structure of a sentence. A common error in word usage occurs when a word's meaning does not fit the context of the sentence. This often occurs with homonyms (words that sound alike but have different meanings).

Incorrect:

Mark likes candy better <u>then</u> gum.

Correct:

Mark likes candy better <u>than</u> gum.

Incorrect:

The dog chased <u>it's</u> tail.

Correct:

The dog chased <u>its</u> tail.

In addition to *than/then* and *it's/its,* some other commonly misused words include *they/their/they're, your/you're, except/accept,* and *affect/effect.*

For contractions (*it's, they're, you're*), you can spell out the contraction to make sure you are using the correct word (*it's* ◗ *it is, they're* ◗ *they are; you're* ◗ *you are*). For other words, however, you will need to learn the correct usage by looking up the word in the dictionary to find out its meaning.

Answering the Writing Skills Questions

Question Types

Now that we have reviewed some common elements of grammar and sentence construction, it is time to look at how those elements are tested on the *ParaPro Assessment*. The questions in the Writing Skills and Knowledge section may appear in four different formats, which are described below.

- You should familiarize yourself with the distinct formats for the questions. This will help save time during the test because you will immediately recognize the kind of information that the question is asking for.

- You will not be required to identify which type of question is being asked, but being aware of the different types of questions is likely to help you answer the questions correctly.

- As you work through the sample questions below, keep track of which kinds of questions you tend to get wrong. While the explanations in the sample questions should help you understand the grammatical rule that is being violated, it may be helpful to seek additional explanations and practice in the review course above or in an up-to-date writing handbook.

1 Sentence-error questions

Sentence-error questions ask you to read a sentence that contains four underlined parts. For each sentence, you must determine which underlined part contains an error. You do not have to identify what type of error it is, nor do you have to suggest how to correct the error. Every sentence contains only *one* underlined error. The sentences that are used in sentence-error questions are sentences you would encounter in books, magazines, and newspapers published for a general reading audience.

The errors in the sentences often involve the following (this list is not exhaustive):

- Subject-verb agreement

- Verb tense

- Parallelism

- Punctuation

- Noun-pronoun agreement

- Errors in word usage

Strategies for answering sentence-error questions:

■ Before you choose an answer, be sure to look at all parts of the sentence to see how they fit together.

■ Sometimes the underlined part consists of a single word; sometimes you must consider more than one word. Where an underlined part is several words long, not all of the elements underlined have to be wrong for that part to be incorrect. The error may depend on only one word or element in the underlined part.

■ An underlined part may be right if read on its own but wrong because of other elements in the sentence. This often happens with agreement errors such as noun-pronoun agreement and subject-verb agreement.

Example:

Although the school board voted unanimously to renovate the classroom, they did not agree
   (A)   (B)   (C)   (D)

about what the new classroom should look like.

In this sentence, the use of the word "they" (C) is incorrect; it is an error in noun-pronoun agreement. Because the noun that the pronoun is standing in for—"the school board"—is singular, the pronoun should also be singular ("it" instead of "they").

■ If you see a line under a blank space, it means that you are to decide whether a punctuation mark (a comma, a semicolon, or an apostrophe) is needed:

Example:

The town mayor, who is also a prominent lawyer specializing in environmental issues __
                                                      (A)   (B)

oversaw the implementation of the town's new recycling program.
  (C)   (D)

This sentence represents an error in comma usage; a comma is needed after "environmental issues" (B). The phrase "who is also a prominent lawyer specializing in environmental issues" is not essential to the meaning of the sentence and needs to be set off from the rest of the sentence by commas before and after it.

- If you see a line under a single punctuation mark, you must consider three possibilities:

1. No punctuation is needed in that spot.

2. Some punctuation mark is needed, but not the one shown.

3. The punctuation mark is correct.

Example:

Texas is home <u>to</u> many varieties of flowers <u>,</u> yellow roses and bluebells <u>are</u> among the most
       (A)   (B)   (C)

popular <u>flowers</u> found in Texas.
    (D)

This is an example of a sentence in which a punctuation mark is needed, but the one shown is not correct. The underlined comma, (B), joins together two independent clauses (clauses that can stand alone). Therefore a semicolon, not a comma, is needed to make the sentence correct.

- If you think that an underlined section contains an error, try correcting the error mentally in one of the following ways. Remember, the question does not ask you to correct the error; this is just one way of making sure that the answer you have chosen is the right one.

1. *You can delete an element.* You may need to delete the entire underlined portion, or you may need to delete only part of the underlined portion to make the sentence correct. For example, the phrase "had been running" may be incorrect because in the context of the sentence it should say simply, "running."

2. *You can change the form of an element that is already there.* For example, you could change the possessive "bird's" to the plural "birds."

3. *You can replace an element.* For example, the singular pronoun "her" may need to be replaced with the plural pronoun "their."

4. *You can add an element.* This may be the case when a space is underlined or when you need to add a word to go with an underlined word. For example, you may need to change "climbed" to "had climbed."

Let's Try It!

Now let's work through some sample questions using the skills and strategies you have learned on the previous pages.

1. The popularity of ginseng supplements and products <u>have increased</u> , <u>despite</u> the <u>lack of</u>
                                             (A)   (B)   (C)

   scientific proof that ginseng <u>has</u> medicinal powers.
                                (D)

Answer

This sentence presents a problem in subject-verb agreement. The word "popularity" is singular (refers to one thing), so it requires a singular verb at (A) to go with it. The correct singular verb is "has increased." As explained in the expert tips above, only the first word of the underlined phrase is incorrect.

2. Although the hippopotamus, Earth's second-largest terrestrial mammal __ <u>looms</u> large in the
                                                             (A) (B)

   popular imagination, <u>surprisingly</u> little <u>is known</u> about it.
                             (C)   (D)

Answer

This sentence presents a problem with punctuation. The phrase "Earth's second-largest terrestrial mammal" is a phrase that gives additional information about the hippopotamus that is not essential to the meaning of the sentence. Such phrases are set off from the rest of the sentence by commas. In the sentence above, the second comma is missing; it should appear at (A). Therefore the answer is (A).

3. <u>Blessed with</u> altitude, dry weather, and clear, dark skies <u>,</u> Arizona is <u>rapid</u> becoming the most
      (A)   (B)   (C)

   popular location for amateur astronomers <u>interested</u> in stargazing.
                                          (D)

Answer

This sentence presents a problem in word form. The word "rapid" provides more information about the verb phrase "is becoming"; it shows that the "becoming" is happening rapidly. Since the word "rapid" is modifying a verb, it is behaving as an adverb and should appear in the form of an adverb. To put "rapid" in adverb form, add -*ly*. The correct word would be "rapidly." The answer is (C).

2 Parts-of-sentence questions

Parts-of-sentence questions provide you with a sentence and then ask you to identify a word or phrase in the sentence as a particular part of a sentence. The parts of sentences you may be asked to identify are:

- the subject

- the simple predicate (verb)

 Expert tips:

- Remember that subjects and predicates can be separated from each other by other parts of the sentence.

    Example:

    The superhero, who fought crime at night, always slept during the day.

    In this sentence, the subject ("superhero") is separated from the simple predicate (the verb that tells what the subject does—in this case, "slept") by the phrase "who fought crime at night."

- Remember that a sentence may contain two or more clauses that each contains a noun and a verb. Be sure to choose only the subject and simple predicate that together represent the main doer and the main action of the sentence.

    Example:

    The rabbit, the one that lives in the bushes, ate all of the carrots in the garden.

    The main action of the sentence is the rabbit eating the carrots. The subject of the sentence is "rabbit" and the simple predicate is "ate." Although the clause "the one that lives in the bushes" contains a noun and a verb, it represents only supporting information that is not essential to understanding the main action of the sentence.

Let's Try It!

Now let's work through some sample questions using the skills and strategies you have learned on the previous page.

4. For more than half a century, California has led the nation in agricultural output.

    What is the <u>subject</u> of the sentence above?

    (A) century
    (B) California
    (C) nation
    (D) output

Answer

To find the subject, first identify the verb in the sentence and then ask the question "*Who* is performing this action?" The verb in this sentence is "has led." Answering the question "*Who* has led?" leads you to the answer "California" (B).

5. On September 5, 1882, when some 10,000 workers assembled in New York City, America experienced its first Labor Day parade.

    What is the <u>simple predicate</u> (the verb that tells what the subject does) in the sentence above?

    (A) On
    (B) when
    (C) assembled
    (D) experienced

Answer

(A) and (B) are not verbs, so they can be ruled out immediately. (C) is a verb, but it is a verb from an introductory element ("when some 10,000 assembled in New York City") that does not contain the subject of the sentence. (D) is a verb, and it is the verb in the sentence that explains what the subject (America) is doing. Therefore, (D) is the simple predicate.

3 Parts-of-speech questions

Parts of speech questions provide you with a sentence and then ask you to identify a word in the sentence as a particular part of speech. You may be asked to identify these parts of speech:

■ noun

■ verb

■ adjective

■ adverb

■ pronoun

■ preposition

 Expert tips:

■ Look for common characteristics of different parts of speech. For example, adverbs often (but not always) end in -*ly*.

■ If you are having trouble identifying the part of speech of the underlined word, try identifying the parts of speech for some of the other words in the sentence. Since all of the words in the sentence are related to one another (e.g., nouns perform the actions of the verbs), this may help you figure out the part of speech of the underlined word.

Let's Try It!

Now let's work through a sample question using the skills and strategies you have learned on the previous page.

6. Although Billie Holiday had no formal musical training, she became one of the greatest jazz singers of all <u>time</u>, and her recordings are now regarded as masterpieces.

In the sentence above, the underlined word is being used as

(A) a noun
(B) a verb
(C) an adjective
(D) an adverb

Answer

To answer this question, identify what the underlined word *does*. Use the following questions to guide you.

➤ Does it name a person, place, thing or concept? Then it is a noun.

➤ Does it name an action? Then it is a verb.

➤ Does it describe a noun? Then it is an adjective.

➤ Does it describe a verb? Then it is an adverb.

In this question, the word "time" names a concept. Therefore, answer (A), a noun, is correct.

4 Spelling questions

Spelling questions ask you to identify which word from a list of four words is NOT spelled correctly. You need only to identify the word that has the error; you do not have to provide the correct spelling. Spelling is a skill that is developed over time through careful reading and writing. However, it may help to review the common spelling rules listed below.

 Expert tips:

- Pay careful attention to the spelling of plural words: most plural words are formed by adding *-s* or *-es* to the singular form. Some words, however, change their spelling when they are made plural (examples: *leaf* ▶ *leaves*; *tomato* ▶ *tomatoes*).

- Look out for words that contain sounds that can be spelled in more than one way. For example, the word *vertical* could be misspelled as *verticle*.

- Watch out for words that need doubled consonants to preserve short vowel sounds in the root word. For example, the word *referring* needs two *r*'s to preserve the sound of the root word *refer*.

- Keep in mind common spelling rules for vowels, such as "*i* before *e* except after *c*."

- Review the rules for verbs that end in *y*: verbs that end in a consonant + *y* often change their form (*try, tries, trying, tried*), while verbs that end in a vowel + *y* don't change as much (*play, plays, playing, played*).

- Keep in mind the rules for spelling for suffixes. For example: keep a silent *-e* before an *-ly* suffix (*time, timely*); keep a silent *-e* before a suffix beginning with a consonant (*fate, fateful*); drop a silent *-e* before a suffix beginning with a vowel (*love, loving*), etc.

Let's Try It!

Now let's work through a sample question using the skills and strategies you have learned on the previous page.

7. Which word is NOT spelled correctly?

   (A) likely
   (B) justifiable
   (C) rateing
   (D) stopped

The word "rating" should be spelled without the *e*. The spelling for this word follows the rule discussed in the final bullet on the previous page: its silent *-e* should be dropped before adding a suffix that begins with a vowel (*-ing*). The correct answer is (C).

You will find more sample questions as part of the complete practice test in chapter 7.

Part II: Application of Writing Skills and Knowledge to Classroom Instruction

Writing Application questions are typically based on classroom scenarios in which students are planning, composing, revising, or editing documents written for a variety of purposes. Some of the skills and knowledge you used in the Writing Skills and Knowledge section of the *ParaPro Assessment*, such as identifying errors in grammar, punctuation, and word choice, will be useful in answering Writing Application questions. The Writing Application questions also draw on other knowledge and skills related to writing, such as using outlines, developing main ideas for paragraphs, and using appropriate language.

What's Being Tested?

Some Writing Application questions concern aspects of the *writing process*, the full range of activities used when composing written documents. These questions measure your ability to help students

- use prewriting to generate and organize ideas (including freewriting and using outlines)

- identify and use appropriate reference materials

- draft and revise (including composing or refining a thesis statement, writing focused and organized paragraphs, and writing a conclusion)

- edit written documents for clarity, grammar, sentence integrity (run-ons and sentence fragments), word usage, punctuation, and spelling

Other questions are concerned with *writing applications*, the application of writing for different purposes. These questions measure your ability to help students

- write for different purposes and audiences

- recognize and write in different modes and forms (e.g., descriptive essays, persuasive essays, narratives, letters)

It may be helpful to review an up-to-date writing handbook. Many writing handbooks have a section devoted to the writing process, as well as sections devoted to identifying and correcting sentence-level errors. On the following pages are some key elements of the writing process and writing applications that you should keep in mind as you prepare for the test.

REVIEW COURSE: Writing Application

Writers use a wide variety of strategies and approaches. Below are some of the more common approaches to writing, especially those used by students in the classroom. These approaches are oriented toward helping students learn how to develop their writing skills. Thus the approaches listed below are describing the *activities* that a writer engages in to write clearly and persuasively, rather than describing a *formula* for the ideal student paper. Play close attention to the activities—the actions a writer takes—as you review the strategies below for defining and organizing a topic, drafting, and revising.

Before writers even begin drafting their papers, they must have a clear (if often unwritten) idea of three things: a topic about which to write, a purpose for writing, and an intended audience.

Defining a topic

Writers must identify a specific focus for their papers. For example, if a writer begins by looking at the causes of the American Revolution but then suddenly begins writing about generals of the Civil War, the reader may become confused. By limiting a topic to one specific subject or set of ideas, the writer presents only the details that support that topic. This enables the reader to follow the writer's ideas about the topic.

Defining a purpose

The writer must identify a goal: what the writer wants to accomplish and/or how the writer wants to affect the reader. Here are some common purposes for writing:

- *To summarize:*

  Summaries describe another piece of writing or an event in relatively few words and sentences. Summaries provide information about main events and ideas and tend to omit details that are not significant.

- *To describe:*

  Descriptive writing provides readers with an understanding of an object, a person, a place, or a series of events. Descriptive writing can be richly detailed and in some cases is intended to evoke an emotional response from the reader. Descriptive writing, however, does not attempt to persuade the reader to believe in a particular idea or take a specific action.

- *To instruct:*

  Instructive writing explains how the reader should *do* something. It often provides step-by-step instructions for achieving a goal.

- *To persuade:*

  Persuasive writing urges the reader to take a particular position on an issue or prompts the reader to take a specific action. Examples of persuasive writing include newspaper editorials and letters to elected representatives.

Defining an audience

Defining an audience helps writers to determine the appropriate vocabulary and tone (often the choice is between formal or informal) to use in a specific piece of writing. For example, a more formal tone would be appropriate to use when writing to someone of authority, such as the president of a company, a school principal, or a government official. A more informal tone is appropriate for writing that would be read by close friends and family.

After defining a topic, purpose, and audience, writers often engage in a variety of *prewriting activities* that help them develop and organize their ideas. There are many different kinds of prewriting activities, but here are some of the more common ones:

- *Freewriting:*

  When writers have difficulty figuring out what to write about a topic, freewriting can help them develop some initial ideas. Writers freewrite by writing whatever comes into their mind about a topic for a set amount of time (often as little as five to ten minutes). Once they start writing, they should not stop; the idea is not to worry about making mistakes. The writing that is produced as a result is often informal and tentative; however, it can often be usefully revised for inclusion in a paper.

- *Brainstorming:*

  Brainstorming is another form of freewriting. Instead of writing complete sentences, writers make a list of ideas that they might want to include in their writing. Brainstorming lists can be used to help organize a paper; writers can rearrange items on the list to produce a more effective organization.

- *Mapping or clustering:*

  Mapping, also known as clustering, can be helpful when writers have a lot of ideas that they need to organize. They write down a word or phrase that describes the topic in the center of a blank sheet of paper. Then they write down related ideas and connect them to the topic and to one another by drawing lines. The result is a visual "map" that writers can then use to organize their ideas.

- *Outlining:*

  Outlines offer a more formal, step-by-step description of each idea as it will appear in the writer's paper. For example, the main idea of a paragraph could be represented as one point of an outline, and the idea for each sentence in the paragraph could be a sub-point under that main idea.

After developing and planning their work, writers create a first draft. The goal of the first draft usually is to develop ideas by creating clear, coherent paragraphs.

Paragraphs

Writers need to learn to write paragraphs that are unified—developed around a single idea that is supported by details specific to that idea. Common skills used to build strong paragraphs include the following:

- Expressing the main idea of the paragraph in a *topic sentence*:

  The topic sentence of a paragraph contains the main idea of the paragraph—the concept to which all of the other sentences in the paragraph will refer. A strong topic sentence is clear and concise and serves as an introduction to the rest of the paragraph. Writers can begin developing topic sentences by answering the following question: "What is the one idea I want readers to understand as a result of reading this paragraph?"

- Including appropriate *supporting details*:

  Determining which ideas are appropriate to include within a single paragraph is a two-step process. First, the writer must determine the main idea or argument for the paragraph. Then the writer must determine if the supporting detail contributes to that main idea or argument. Here is an example:

Main idea:

"Migrating birds follow the same routes every year as they fly south for the winter."

Appropriate supporting detail:
"Geese that live in Canada during the summer use a route that takes them over the Mississippi river." This detail fits into the paragraph because it provides a *specific example of the main idea*; it describes a specific kind of bird using a specific flight route.

Inappropriate supporting detail:
"Canada geese can be recognized by their dark bills." This detail does not fit into the paragraph because the idea is not connected to the main topic—the migration patterns of birds.

- Creating *new paragraphs*: A paragraph should not have more than one idea or topic. If a paragraph has more than one idea or topic, it should be divided into two paragraphs.

Using reference materials

Sometimes writers need extra information in order to complete their writing assignments, and they consult reference materials to find that information. Reference materials could include newspapers, encyclopedias, magazines, general interest books, reference books on specific topics, and Web sites. Use the following suggestions for choosing reference materials:

- *Locating general information about a topic:*

  Look for sources that provide a broad range of information about a topic. Such reference sources include encyclopedias, general-interest books about the topic, and some Web sites.

- *Finding information about current events and issues:*

  Look for sources that provide up-to-date information and news, such as newspapers and magazine articles that appear in print or on the Internet.

- *Finding information about a topic that requires specialized knowledge:*

  Look for resources that provide detailed, in-depth information and specialized knowledge. Such resources include reference books and topic-specific books (books on particular areas of history, geography, biography, etc.).

Proofreading and editing sentences

Another key aspect of the writing process is proofreading—identifying errors in grammar and sentence structure that will interfere with the clarity of the writing. You can use many of the techniques you developed for the Writing Skills and Knowledge section to help you recognize errors in punctuation, word usage, and spelling. Other common sentence-level errors include the following:

- *Run-on, or fused, sentences:*

  Run-on sentences (also known as fused sentences) are two complete sentences that are run together without any punctuation between them, or with a comma between them but no coordinating conjunction (such as *and, but, or*). Remember that a complete sentence is one with a subject and a verb that can stand alone; writing handbooks refer to these as independent clauses. Check for run-on sentences whenever a sentence has two or more independent clauses to make sure that the independent clauses are separated by appropriate punctuation or conjunctions.

  Here are examples of run-on sentences:

  Incorrect:

  Some dinosaurs ate only meat other dinosaurs ate only vegetables.

  (This sentence is incorrect because it consists of two independent clauses that are run together without punctuation or a coordinating conjunction.)

  Correct:

  Some dinosaurs ate only meat. Other dinosaurs ate only vegetables.

  (You can separate clauses into two sentences by adding a period.)

  Some dinosaurs ate only meat, <u>but</u> other dinosaurs ate only vegetables.

  (You also can add a comma and a coordinating conjunction.)

  Incorrect:

  I like to eat spinach on pizza, I do not like it by itself.

  (This sentence contains two independent clauses: "I like to eat spinach on pizza" and "I do not like it by itself." A comma is not sufficient to separate the two independent clauses.)

Correct:

I like to eat spinach on pizza, <u>but</u> I do not like it by itself.

(You can correct the sentence by adding a coordinating conjunction.)

- *Sentence fragments:*

  Sentence fragments are phrases that are punctuated as if they were sentences but that are missing a key element of a sentence. All sentences must contain a subject and a predicate. Check to make sure that each sentence contains both of these elements. Sometimes sentence fragments are noticeable because they are especially short. Below are some examples of sentence fragments.

  Incorrect:

  Rode her bicycle to the store.

  (This sentence fragment is missing a subject.)

  Correct:

  <u>Katie</u> rode her bicycle to the store.

  (The sentence fragment has been corrected by adding a subject.)

  Incorrect:

  Todd, the best swimmer in the school.

  (This sentence fragment is missing a verb.)

  Correct:

  Todd <u>is</u> the best swimmer in the school.

  (The sentence fragment has been corrected by adding the verb.)

Incorrect:

Although Curtis ate breakfast.

(Even though this example contains both a subject, *Curtis*, and a verb, *ate*, it is still a sentence fragment because the word *although* signals an upcoming contrast that is never fulfilled.)

Correct:

Although Curtis ate breakfast, <u>he was hungry by 10 A.M.</u>

(The sentence fragment has been corrected by supplying the missing part of the sentence.)

Answering the Writing Application Questions

Here are some general test-taking tips for Writing Application questions.

- You can use your reading skills to help you become a better writer. Use any general reading you already do (such as magazines, newspapers, Internet sites) as an opportunity to practice skills for the exam. As you read, practice defining the main idea, purpose, and intended audience of the piece of writing.

- Develop a deeper understanding of the writing process by trying to relate some of the prewriting, writing, and revising practices to your own writing. Think about how you compose letters of request to businesses (such as banks or health insurance companies) or family newsletters. How do you use prewriting, composing, and revising techniques similar to the ones described above?

Let's Try It!

Now let's work through some sample questions using the skills and strategies you have learned from the previous examples.

Question 8 is based on the following rough draft written by a student.

Growing Tomatoes
by Nick F.

(1) You will need a small plot of land. (2) You can buy young plants at a garden store, or even at a discount store. (3) Dig a small hole for each plant, at least a foot apart. (4) Remove the tomato plant from the pot and put it in the hole. (5) Put back the soil. (6) Now, water your plants and be patient. (7) The tomatoes are going to taste much better than ones from the store!

8. Nick wants to begin his paper with a sentence that introduces his main idea. What would be the strongest first sentence for Nick's paper?

   (A) Tomatoes do not grow well in very sandy soil.
   (B) Tomato plants do not cost that much to buy.
   (C) You have to follow a few steps to grow tomatoes in your garden.
   (D) If it doesn't rain, your tomato plants won't do well.

Answer

To answer this question, you have to figure out what the main idea of the paragraph is. Look for the answer choice that connects all of the sentences in the paragraph together. Since all of the sentences describe the steps involved in growing tomatoes, choice (C) is the best answer.

Questions 9–10 are based on the following letter written by a student.

Dear School Superintendent:

(1) I would like to convince you that high school should begin at 9:00 A.M. rather than at 8:00 A.M. (2) I will tell you why. (3) At last, research has shown what we teenagers have known for a long time; we are tired, too tired to really concentrate in school. (4) Recently, research found that teenagers need more sleep than younger children. (5) In order for us teenagers not to be tired, we need about 9 hours and 15 minutes of sleep to feel truly rested. (6) This is different than elementary school students who need only 8 hours of sleep.

Sincerely,
Stella

---

9. Which sentence could Stella add to her letter as additional support for her main idea?

   (A) I go to bed too late to be awake during my first-period class.
   (B) Studies have found that in districts where high school classes begin at 9:00 A.M., students pay more attention in class.
   (C) Data from attendance records show that high school students tend to be late to school more often in the spring than in the fall.
   (D) High school students who don't have much homework are more likely to sign up for after-school activities.

Answer

This question requires you to make two steps. First, you must identify the argument that Stella is making in her letter. Then you need to find the statement that provides the most support for that argument. In her letter, Stella argues that high school classes should begin at 9 A.M. rather than at 8 A.M. She supports her argument by citing research indicating that teenagers are too tired to concentrate in school unless they get a certain amount of sleep. Choice (B) is correct because it provides further support for her argument: research indicates that in places where school starts at 9 A.M., students are better able to pay attention in class. Choice (A) is incorrect because in making a personal statement about the time she goes to bed, Stella fails to support her argument that classes should start later for all high school students. Choice (C) is incorrect because it does not relate the issue of lateness to the time when school should start. Choice (D) is incorrect because it focuses on a different issue than Stella does.

10. The primary purpose of Stella's letter is to

   (A) summarize
   (B) describe
   (C) instruct
   (D) persuade

Answer

Look again at the paragraph for an indication of the purpose of Stella's letter. In the first sentence, she claims that she wants to "convince" the superintendent of her idea. Convincing is a form of persuading, so choice (D), persuade, is most appropriate.

Questions 11–12 are based on the following short essay written by Brian.

In his essay, Brian discusses the effects of captivity on wild animals.

(1) At the zoo we saw many species that we studied in science class. (2) For example, chimpanzees and polar bears. (3) Some of these animals benefit from living in captivity. (4) In the wild, chimps only live to be about twenty the chimp we saw at the zoo was 34 years old. (5) Baby polar bears are often attacked by males in the wild, but in the zoo, males are rarely mean to the cubs or females. (6) However, captivity has drawbacks as well. (7) Many of the animals suffer from tooth decay because visitors feed them bad food. (8) Also, the caged animals seemed depressed to me.

11. Brian wants to divide his essay into two paragraphs, one for each main idea. Which sentence should be the opening sentence for the second paragraph?

   (A) Sentence 4
   (B) Sentence 5
   (C) Sentence 6
   (D) Sentence 7

Answer

This question asks you to consider how ideas should be organized in paragraphs. You need to determine what Brian's ideas are and where he stops discussing one idea and begins discussing another. Brian is discussing both the benefits and the drawbacks to animals of living in captivity. In sentences 3 through 5, he discusses the benefits of captivity. Sentence 6 marks the place that he shifts to discussing the drawbacks. Therefore, the correct answer is (C).

12. Brian often has trouble identifying errors in his own work, especially run-on sentences (two sentences fused together without proper punctuation) and sentence fragments (incomplete sentences). Which TWO sentences in his essay contain such errors?

    (A) Sentences 1 and 6
    (B) Sentences 2 and 4
    (C) Sentences 3 and 7
    (D) Sentences 5 and 8

Answer

This question asks you to identify two different problems with sentence structure: run-ons and sentence fragments. Run-ons often contain two independent clauses (clauses consisting of a subject and verb pair that can stand alone as a complete sentence) that are not separated by punctuation or commas and conjunctions. Sentences 4 and 5 both have two independent clauses. In sentence 5, the independent clauses are separated by a comma and conjunction ("but"), as they should be. In sentence 4, however, the independent clauses are not separated. Thus, sentence 4 is a run-on. To find sentence fragments, look for sentences that are missing a subject, a verb, or an entire independent clause. Sentence 2 is missing a verb. Since sentence 2 is a sentence fragment and sentence 4 is a run-on sentence, the answer is (B).

You will find more sample questions as part of the complete practice test in chapter 7.

Glossary of Important Terms Used in This Chapter

Remember, for the *ParaPro Assessment* you are **not** expected to be able to define all of these terms. This glossary is provided only to help you follow the discussion in the chapter. Special grammar terms are used in the chapter in case you want to consult a grammar handbook for more help. It is often easier to find more information about particular grammar concepts if you know what they are called.

Term	Definition
adjective	a part of speech: a word that modifies (describes) a noun or pronoun
adverb	a part of speech: a word that modifies a verb, an adjective, another adverb, or a clause; often ends in *-ly*
agreement	a rule of grammar that requires certain words in a sentence to share the same properties, such as number
apostrophe	a mark (') used to show that a noun belongs to someone or something; also used in place of letters that are dropped in contractions, such as "I'm" and "can't"
clause	a group of words that contains both a subject and a verb
comma	a mark (,) that separates elements of a sentence; may separate a series of words in a list or two separate clauses
complete predicate	a part of a sentence: it includes both the main verb and the person or thing receiving the action of the verb; may also include adverbs, adjectives, prepositions, and prepositional phrases
conjunction	a part of speech: a word that joins together two parts of a sentence (such as *and*, *but*, *or*)
contraction	a word formed by omitting some letters from a pair of words, such as *we're* and *haven't*
dependent clause	a clause (has both a subject and a verb) that depends upon another part of the sentence to clarify its meaning; it cannot stand alone as a complete sentence

fused sentence	see *run-on sentence*
independent clause	a clause (has both a subject and a verb) that does not depend on another part of the sentence to clarify its meaning; it can stand alone as a complete sentence
interjection	a part of speech: a word that expresses emotion; may be inserted into a sentence or stand alone; usually is punctuated by an exclamation point
nonrestrictive phrase, clause, or word	a phrase, clause, or word that provides additional information that is not essential to the meaning of the sentence; it modifies a subject or object but is not necessary to identify that subject or object; surrounded by commas or parentheses
noun	a part of speech: a word that names a person, place, thing, or concept
noun-pronoun agreement	a rule of grammar that requires pronouns to indicate the same number as the nouns to which they refer; the noun and pronoun both must be singular, or both must be plural
parallelism	a rule of grammar that requires a series of items in a sentence to be in similar form; clarifies the relationship among the parts of the sentence
personal pronoun	a pronoun that stands in for a noun (such as *I, we, me, him*)
possessive pronoun	a pronoun that refers to a noun (such as *my, our, yours, his*)
predicate	a part of a sentence: the action that the subject performs or an assertion about that subject
preposition	a part of speech: a word used most often in front of a noun or pronoun that identifies a relationship such as time or space
pronoun	a part of speech: a word that stands in for or refers to a noun (see also *personal pronoun* and *possessive pronoun*)
proper noun	a noun that gives the name of a specific person, place, thing, or concept; always capitalized

run-on sentence	a sentence that is erroneously formed by fusing two complete sentences without any punctuation between them, or with a comma between them but no coordinating conjunction (such as *and*, *but*, *or*); sometimes called a fused sentence
semicolon	a mark (;) that separates two independent clauses that are closely related in subject matter; also used in place of commas to separate items in a list when the items themselves are phrases that contain commas
sentence	a unit of grammar that can stand by itself; normally contains at least a subject and a predicate
sentence fragment	a phrase that is punctuated as if it were a sentence but that is missing a key element of a sentence (often a subject or a predicate)
simple predicate	a part of a sentence: it consists only of the main verb in the sentence and is always the main verb
subject	a part of a sentence: the person, place, or thing that is performing an action; can be a word (common noun, proper noun, or pronoun), phrase, clause, or combination of nouns
subject-verb agreement	a rule of grammar that requires the subjects and verbs of a sentence to indicate the same number; the subject and verb both must be singular, or both must be plural
verb	a part of speech: a word that tells what a subject does or is
verb tense agreement	a rule of grammar that requires the verbs of a sentence to have the same tense (e.g., past tense, present tense) if they are referring to events that happen at the same time

Chapter 7
Complete Practice Test

▶ ▶ ▶ ▶ ▶ ▶ ▶ ▶ ▶ ▶ ▶ ▶

Now that you have reviewed the knowledge and skills you will need for the reading, writing, and math questions, you should take the following practice test. You will probably find it helpful to simulate actual testing conditions, giving yourself about 150 minutes to work on the questions. You can cut out and use the answer sheet provided if you wish.

Keep in mind that the test you take at an actual administration will have different questions, although the proportion of questions in each area and major subarea will be approximately the same. You should not expect the percentage of questions you answer correctly in these practice questions to be exactly the same as when you take the test at an actual administration, since numerous factors affect a person's performance in any given testing situation.

When you have finished the practice questions, you can score your answers and read the explanations of the best answer choices in chapter 8.

Professional Assessments for Beginning Teachers®

TEST NAME:

ParaPro Assessment

Practice Questions

Time—150 Minutes
90 Questions

DO NOT USE INK

Use only a pencil with soft black lead (No. 2 or HB) to complete this answer sheet.
Be sure to fill in completely the oval that corresponds to the proper letter or number.
Completely erase any errors or stray marks.

THE PRAXIS SERIES
Professional Assessments for Beginning Teachers®

Answer Sheet C

PAGE 1

2.

YOUR NAME: _____
(Print)
Last Name (Family or Surname)   First Name (Given)   M. I.

MAILING ADDRESS: _____
(Print)
P.O. Box or Street Address   Apt. # (If any)

City   State or Province

Country   Zip or Postal Code

TELEPHONE NUMBER: (___) _____   (___) _____
Home   Business

SIGNATURE: _____   **TEST DATE:** _____

1. NAME
Enter your last name and first initial.
Omit spaces, hyphens, apostrophes, etc.

Last Name (first 6 letters)   F I

(A)(B)(C)(D)(E)(F)(G)(H)(I)(J)(K)(L)(M)(N)(O)(P)(Q)(R)(S)(T)(U)(V)(W)(X)(Y)(Z)

3. DATE OF BIRTH

Month	Day
Jan.	
Feb.	
Mar.	
April	
May	
June	
July	
Aug.	
Sept.	
Oct.	
Nov.	
Dec.	

4. SOCIAL SECURITY NUMBER

5. CANDIDATE ID NUMBER

6. TEST CENTER / REPORTING LOCATION

Center Number   Room Number

Center Name

City   State or Province

Country

7. TEST CODE / FORM CODE

0
1

8. TEST BOOK SERIAL NUMBER

9. TEST FORM

10. TEST NAME

Educational Testing Service, ETS, the ETS logo, and THE PRAXIS SERIES:PROFESSIONAL ASSESSMENTS FOR BEGINNING TEACHERS and its logo are registered trademarks of Educational Testing Service.

ETS Educational Testing Service

51055 • 08920 • TF71M500   Q2573-06
MH01159

I.N. 202974

1 2 3 4

CERTIFICATION STATEMENT: (Please write the following statement below. DO NOT PRINT.)
"I hereby agree to the conditions set forth in the *Registration Bulletin* and certify that I am the person whose name and address appear on this answer sheet."

_____

_____

_____

SIGNATURE: _____ DATE: _____ / _____ / _____

Month   Day   Year

BE SURE EACH MARK IS DARK AND COMPLETELY FILLS THE INTENDED SPACE AS ILLUSTRATED HERE: ●

1–40	41–80	81–120	121–160
1 Ⓐ Ⓑ Ⓒ Ⓓ	41 Ⓐ Ⓑ Ⓒ Ⓓ	81 Ⓐ Ⓑ Ⓒ Ⓓ	121 Ⓐ Ⓑ Ⓒ Ⓓ
2 Ⓐ Ⓑ Ⓒ Ⓓ	42 Ⓐ Ⓑ Ⓒ Ⓓ	82 Ⓐ Ⓑ Ⓒ Ⓓ	122 Ⓐ Ⓑ Ⓒ Ⓓ
3 Ⓐ Ⓑ Ⓒ Ⓓ	43 Ⓐ Ⓑ Ⓒ Ⓓ	83 Ⓐ Ⓑ Ⓒ Ⓓ	123 Ⓐ Ⓑ Ⓒ Ⓓ
4 Ⓐ Ⓑ Ⓒ Ⓓ	44 Ⓐ Ⓑ Ⓒ Ⓓ	84 Ⓐ Ⓑ Ⓒ Ⓓ	124 Ⓐ Ⓑ Ⓒ Ⓓ
5 Ⓐ Ⓑ Ⓒ Ⓓ	45 Ⓐ Ⓑ Ⓒ Ⓓ	85 Ⓐ Ⓑ Ⓒ Ⓓ	125 Ⓐ Ⓑ Ⓒ Ⓓ
6 Ⓐ Ⓑ Ⓒ Ⓓ	46 Ⓐ Ⓑ Ⓒ Ⓓ	86 Ⓐ Ⓑ Ⓒ Ⓓ	126 Ⓐ Ⓑ Ⓒ Ⓓ
7 Ⓐ Ⓑ Ⓒ Ⓓ	47 Ⓐ Ⓑ Ⓒ Ⓓ	87 Ⓐ Ⓑ Ⓒ Ⓓ	127 Ⓐ Ⓑ Ⓒ Ⓓ
8 Ⓐ Ⓑ Ⓒ Ⓓ	48 Ⓐ Ⓑ Ⓒ Ⓓ	88 Ⓐ Ⓑ Ⓒ Ⓓ	128 Ⓐ Ⓑ Ⓒ Ⓓ
9 Ⓐ Ⓑ Ⓒ Ⓓ	49 Ⓐ Ⓑ Ⓒ Ⓓ	89 Ⓐ Ⓑ Ⓒ Ⓓ	129 Ⓐ Ⓑ Ⓒ Ⓓ
10 Ⓐ Ⓑ Ⓒ Ⓓ	50 Ⓐ Ⓑ Ⓒ Ⓓ	90 Ⓐ Ⓑ Ⓒ Ⓓ	130 Ⓐ Ⓑ Ⓒ Ⓓ
11 Ⓐ Ⓑ Ⓒ Ⓓ	51 Ⓐ Ⓑ Ⓒ Ⓓ	91 Ⓐ Ⓑ Ⓒ Ⓓ	131 Ⓐ Ⓑ Ⓒ Ⓓ
12 Ⓐ Ⓑ Ⓒ Ⓓ	52 Ⓐ Ⓑ Ⓒ Ⓓ	92 Ⓐ Ⓑ Ⓒ Ⓓ	132 Ⓐ Ⓑ Ⓒ Ⓓ
13 Ⓐ Ⓑ Ⓒ Ⓓ	53 Ⓐ Ⓑ Ⓒ Ⓓ	93 Ⓐ Ⓑ Ⓒ Ⓓ	133 Ⓐ Ⓑ Ⓒ Ⓓ
14 Ⓐ Ⓑ Ⓒ Ⓓ	54 Ⓐ Ⓑ Ⓒ Ⓓ	94 Ⓐ Ⓑ Ⓒ Ⓓ	134 Ⓐ Ⓑ Ⓒ Ⓓ
15 Ⓐ Ⓑ Ⓒ Ⓓ	55 Ⓐ Ⓑ Ⓒ Ⓓ	95 Ⓐ Ⓑ Ⓒ Ⓓ	135 Ⓐ Ⓑ Ⓒ Ⓓ
16 Ⓐ Ⓑ Ⓒ Ⓓ	56 Ⓐ Ⓑ Ⓒ Ⓓ	96 Ⓐ Ⓑ Ⓒ Ⓓ	136 Ⓐ Ⓑ Ⓒ Ⓓ
17 Ⓐ Ⓑ Ⓒ Ⓓ	57 Ⓐ Ⓑ Ⓒ Ⓓ	97 Ⓐ Ⓑ Ⓒ Ⓓ	137 Ⓐ Ⓑ Ⓒ Ⓓ
18 Ⓐ Ⓑ Ⓒ Ⓓ	58 Ⓐ Ⓑ Ⓒ Ⓓ	98 Ⓐ Ⓑ Ⓒ Ⓓ	138 Ⓐ Ⓑ Ⓒ Ⓓ
19 Ⓐ Ⓑ Ⓒ Ⓓ	59 Ⓐ Ⓑ Ⓒ Ⓓ	99 Ⓐ Ⓑ Ⓒ Ⓓ	139 Ⓐ Ⓑ Ⓒ Ⓓ
20 Ⓐ Ⓑ Ⓒ Ⓓ	60 Ⓐ Ⓑ Ⓒ Ⓓ	100 Ⓐ Ⓑ Ⓒ Ⓓ	140 Ⓐ Ⓑ Ⓒ Ⓓ
21 Ⓐ Ⓑ Ⓒ Ⓓ	61 Ⓐ Ⓑ Ⓒ Ⓓ	101 Ⓐ Ⓑ Ⓒ Ⓓ	141 Ⓐ Ⓑ Ⓒ Ⓓ
22 Ⓐ Ⓑ Ⓒ Ⓓ	62 Ⓐ Ⓑ Ⓒ Ⓓ	102 Ⓐ Ⓑ Ⓒ Ⓓ	142 Ⓐ Ⓑ Ⓒ Ⓓ
23 Ⓐ Ⓑ Ⓒ Ⓓ	63 Ⓐ Ⓑ Ⓒ Ⓓ	103 Ⓐ Ⓑ Ⓒ Ⓓ	143 Ⓐ Ⓑ Ⓒ Ⓓ
24 Ⓐ Ⓑ Ⓒ Ⓓ	64 Ⓐ Ⓑ Ⓒ Ⓓ	104 Ⓐ Ⓑ Ⓒ Ⓓ	144 Ⓐ Ⓑ Ⓒ Ⓓ
25 Ⓐ Ⓑ Ⓒ Ⓓ	65 Ⓐ Ⓑ Ⓒ Ⓓ	105 Ⓐ Ⓑ Ⓒ Ⓓ	145 Ⓐ Ⓑ Ⓒ Ⓓ
26 Ⓐ Ⓑ Ⓒ Ⓓ	66 Ⓐ Ⓑ Ⓒ Ⓓ	106 Ⓐ Ⓑ Ⓒ Ⓓ	146 Ⓐ Ⓑ Ⓒ Ⓓ
27 Ⓐ Ⓑ Ⓒ Ⓓ	67 Ⓐ Ⓑ Ⓒ Ⓓ	107 Ⓐ Ⓑ Ⓒ Ⓓ	147 Ⓐ Ⓑ Ⓒ Ⓓ
28 Ⓐ Ⓑ Ⓒ Ⓓ	68 Ⓐ Ⓑ Ⓒ Ⓓ	108 Ⓐ Ⓑ Ⓒ Ⓓ	148 Ⓐ Ⓑ Ⓒ Ⓓ
29 Ⓐ Ⓑ Ⓒ Ⓓ	69 Ⓐ Ⓑ Ⓒ Ⓓ	109 Ⓐ Ⓑ Ⓒ Ⓓ	149 Ⓐ Ⓑ Ⓒ Ⓓ
30 Ⓐ Ⓑ Ⓒ Ⓓ	70 Ⓐ Ⓑ Ⓒ Ⓓ	110 Ⓐ Ⓑ Ⓒ Ⓓ	150 Ⓐ Ⓑ Ⓒ Ⓓ
31 Ⓐ Ⓑ Ⓒ Ⓓ	71 Ⓐ Ⓑ Ⓒ Ⓓ	111 Ⓐ Ⓑ Ⓒ Ⓓ	151 Ⓐ Ⓑ Ⓒ Ⓓ
32 Ⓐ Ⓑ Ⓒ Ⓓ	72 Ⓐ Ⓑ Ⓒ Ⓓ	112 Ⓐ Ⓑ Ⓒ Ⓓ	152 Ⓐ Ⓑ Ⓒ Ⓓ
33 Ⓐ Ⓑ Ⓒ Ⓓ	73 Ⓐ Ⓑ Ⓒ Ⓓ	113 Ⓐ Ⓑ Ⓒ Ⓓ	153 Ⓐ Ⓑ Ⓒ Ⓓ
34 Ⓐ Ⓑ Ⓒ Ⓓ	74 Ⓐ Ⓑ Ⓒ Ⓓ	114 Ⓐ Ⓑ Ⓒ Ⓓ	154 Ⓐ Ⓑ Ⓒ Ⓓ
35 Ⓐ Ⓑ Ⓒ Ⓓ	75 Ⓐ Ⓑ Ⓒ Ⓓ	115 Ⓐ Ⓑ Ⓒ Ⓓ	155 Ⓐ Ⓑ Ⓒ Ⓓ
36 Ⓐ Ⓑ Ⓒ Ⓓ	76 Ⓐ Ⓑ Ⓒ Ⓓ	116 Ⓐ Ⓑ Ⓒ Ⓓ	156 Ⓐ Ⓑ Ⓒ Ⓓ
37 Ⓐ Ⓑ Ⓒ Ⓓ	77 Ⓐ Ⓑ Ⓒ Ⓓ	117 Ⓐ Ⓑ Ⓒ Ⓓ	157 Ⓐ Ⓑ Ⓒ Ⓓ
38 Ⓐ Ⓑ Ⓒ Ⓓ	78 Ⓐ Ⓑ Ⓒ Ⓓ	118 Ⓐ Ⓑ Ⓒ Ⓓ	158 Ⓐ Ⓑ Ⓒ Ⓓ
39 Ⓐ Ⓑ Ⓒ Ⓓ	79 Ⓐ Ⓑ Ⓒ Ⓓ	119 Ⓐ Ⓑ Ⓒ Ⓓ	159 Ⓐ Ⓑ Ⓒ Ⓓ
40 Ⓐ Ⓑ Ⓒ Ⓓ	80 Ⓐ Ⓑ Ⓒ Ⓓ	120 Ⓐ Ⓑ Ⓒ Ⓓ	160 Ⓐ Ⓑ Ⓒ Ⓓ

FOR ETS USE ONLY	R1	R2	R3	R4	R5	R6	R7	R8	TR	CS

READING

Directions for Questions 1–30: Each of the questions or incomplete statements below is followed by four suggested answers or completions. Select the one that is best in each case and fill in the corresponding lettered space on the answer sheet with a heavy, dark mark so that you cannot see the letter.

1. In 1620 a group of English people crossed the North Atlantic to establish a small colony in what is now called New England. The story of these Pilgrims has become an important part of the history of the United States. At the time, however, the colony was simply part of the spread of European culture. For more than a century, the nations of western Europe had been establishing colonies and trading posts around the world.

    The primary purpose of the passage is to

    (A) describe the experience of daily life in the colony established by the Pilgrims
    (B) explain how several colonies in New England were established and governed
    (C) describe how trade routes between Europe and the United States were developed and how they have changed
    (D) point out that the colony established by the Pilgrims was only one of many European colonies

2. In the United States, the ocelot, a type of wild cat found in Texas, has been an endangered species since 1982. The most important cause of the ocelot's decline is loss of its habitat. Almost 95 percent of the native land cover of south Texas has been altered, and the ocelot has been unable to adapt to the resulting decrease in the thick vegetation that provides it shelter. Hope for the ocelot's survival rests on restoring a portion of south Texas to its natural state.

    The passage suggests that the ocelot needs a habitat that

    (A) provides areas sheltered by plants
    (B) has little variation in temperature
    (C) is home to few other animals
    (D) has been altered by human activities

Questions 3–4 are based on the following passage drawn from a short story by Toni Cade Bambara.

Line

5

10

The puddle had frozen over, and me and Cathy went stompin in it. The twins from next door, Tyrone and Terry, were swingin so high out of sight we forgot we were waitin our turn on the tire. Cathy jumped up and came down hard on her heels and started tap-dancin. And the frozen patch splinterin every which way underneath kinda spooky. "Looks like a plastic spider web," she said. "A sort of weird spider, I guess, with many mental problems." But really it looked like the crystal paperweight Granny kept in the parlor.

3. The excerpt primarily describes children

(A) talking with their grandmother
(B) disagreeing over the rules of a game
(C) ice-skating on a pond
(D) playing outdoors

4. The narrator of the excerpt thinks that the splinters in the frozen puddle are like

(A) tap-dancing steps
(B) a spider web
(C) a crystal paperweight
(D) tire tracks

Questions 5–7 are based on the following passage.

Until the 1970's most literature
Line published by Native American women was
poetry. The publication of Janet Campbell
Hale's *The Owl's Song* (1974) and Leslie
5 Silko's *Ceremony* (1977), however, added
a new genre—the novel—to the body of
literature by Native American women.
Elizabeth Cook's *Then Badger Said This*
(1977) introduced yet another approach, a
10 combination of poetry and prose. As
contemporary Native American women
writers begin to reshape Native American
literature, they no longer express
themselves exclusively in traditional forms.
15 Instead, they are reworking traditional
structures as they continue the process of
articulating Native American experiences.

5. The passage is primarily concerned with

 (A) discussing a novel that strongly influenced
 the work of Native American women
 writers
 (B) describing developments in the Native
 American literary tradition
 (C) challenging a theory about the work of a
 particular Native American author
 (D) contrasting the works of three Native
 American authors

6. In the context of the passage, the word "body"
(line 6) most nearly means

 (A) organization
 (B) size
 (C) human being
 (D) collection

7. The passage suggests that Hale, Silko, and
Cook are

 (A) primarily interested in writing poetry
 (B) helping to reshape Native American
 literature
 (C) better at writing short stories than novels
 (D) working exclusively with traditional
 literary forms

Questions 8–11 are based on the following passage.

Until the recent discovery of two
Line 4,600-year-old ships, most of what was
known about ancient Egyptian ships came
from drawings of ships in the Egyptians'
5 tombs. Water travel was important to the
Egyptians, so they liked to display
drawings of ships in their tombs. Because
Egypt was crisscrossed with little canals,
the Egyptians used papyrus rafts and
10 wooden vessels for transporting people
and goods, as well as for hunting and
fishing. The ancient Egyptians also built
seagoing ships for trade with other
Mediterranean cultures.
15 The two 4,600-year-old wooden
ships—about 142 feet long—that were
recently found at the base of the Great
Pyramid are huge in comparison with
other Egyptian ships. What purpose these
20 ships served remains a mystery to
archaeologists. Why did the ancient
Egyptians take apart and bury two full-
size royal ships at King Khufu's gravesite
at the base of the Great Pyramid? The
25 simplest theory is that the ancient
Egyptians, in keeping with their beliefs,
buried the ships for the dead king's use in
the afterlife. But it was unusual for the
Egyptians to bury full-size ships instead of
30 miniature, symbolic ones. Another theory
about the ships' purpose is that they were
used to carry Khufu's body, by water,
from his palace to his tomb. Marks on the
wood may indicate that the ships had
35 been in water and in motion.

8. The passage suggests that the relationship between ancient Egyptians and their ships is

(A) important but not fully understood by archaeologists
(B) less important than the Egyptians' interest in gold
(C) best understood by studying miniature ships
(D) important primarily for understanding funeral rituals

9. The two 4,600-year-old ships were

(A) used for hunting and fishing
(B) used to transport people across canals
(C) made of papyrus rather than wood
(D) much larger than other ancient Egyptian ships

10. The ancient Egyptians placed drawings of ships in their tombs because

(A) water travel was important in their culture
(B) pictures of the sea were considered a peaceful decoration
(C) there was no room for miniature ships in the tombs
(D) they did not believe in displaying drawings of other objects

11. The author mentions that there were marks on the wood of the 4,600-year-old ships most likely in order to

    (A) explain why the Egyptians buried miniature rather than full-size ships
    (B) indicate support for the theory that the ships were used to carry King Khufu's body
    (C) suggest that the Egyptians buried the ships for King Khufu's use in the afterlife
    (D) explain why the 4,600-year-old ships were taken apart before they were buried

Question 12 is based on the following graph.

ENDANGERED AND THREATENED SPECIES IN THE UNITED STATES

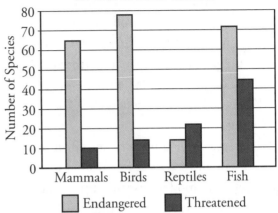

12. The graph can be used to answer which of the following questions?

    (A) Why are more mammal species than fish species considered endangered?
    (B) In what region of the United States are bird species more endangered than reptile species?
    (C) How many reptile species are considered endangered?
    (D) What factors have endangered fish and reptile species?

Questions 13–14 are based on the following passage.

Line   Giant kelp is the largest seaweed in the ocean. Under good conditions, it can grow to a length of 200 feet. Giant kelp also grows faster than any other plant in
5   the ocean world. When these king-size seaweeds grow close together, they form huge kelp beds.

   A kelp bed has a major effect on the ocean and sea creatures around it. It
10   provides food and shelter for countless sea creatures. It also offers them shade from bright light, or a safe place to hide. A kelp bed softens the action of ocean waves, making the water calmer close to shore.

13. Which statement best describes the organization of the second paragraph?

   (A) A problem is described and a possible solution to it is proposed.
   (B) An argument is presented and then proved to be wrong.
   (C) An event is discussed and then contrasted with other events.
   (D) A general statement is made and then supported with evidence.

14. The passage mentions all of the following characteristics of giant kelp EXCEPT its

   (A) size compared to that of other ocean plants
   (B) potential as a food source for humans
   (C) benefits to sea creatures
   (D) effect on the action of waves

15. Accompanied by a small gray spider crawling the dashboard, I drove into the street, around the corner, through the intersection, over the bridge, onto the highway. I was heading toward those little towns that get on the map—if they get on at all—only because some mapmaker has a blank space to fill: Remote, Oregon; Simplicity, Virginia; New Freedom, Pennsylvania; New Hope, Tennessee; Why, Arizona; Whynot, Mississippi. Igo, California (just down the road from Ono), here I come.

The author is primarily concerned with

   (A) pointing out that traveling can be very educational
   (B) explaining the significance of a childhood experience
   (C) describing the methods used to name small towns
   (D) discussing the beginning and destinations of a trip

16. Some of the first movies were based on children's books. By 1920, when movies were still in their infancy, there were four screen versions of *Alice in Wonderland.* There were also three films based on *Robinson Crusoe* and two on *Tom Sawyer.* It seems appropriate that the motion-picture industry in its own youth should turn for inspiration to the literature of childhood.

Which sentence from the passage is most clearly an expression of opinion rather than a statement of fact?

   (A) "Some of…children's books."
   (B) "By 1920,…*in Wonderland.*"
   (C) "There were…*Tom Sawyer.*"
   (D) "It seems…of childhood."

Questions 17–18 are based on the following table of contents from the *Literary History of the United States*.

Literary History of the United States

Table of Contents

17. Chapter 1 is organized by

    (A) theme
    (B) time period
    (C) region
    (D) author

18. To find information about American fiction written around 1765, a reader should start looking on page

    (A) 43
    (B) 49
    (C) 86
    (D) 117

---

19. A student does not understand the meaning of the word "embraced" as it is used in the sentence "After an oil spill polluted the bay near her house, Maria **embraced** the cause of environmental justice, volunteering to campaign for stronger environmental protection laws." The student looks up the word in the dictionary and finds the following definitions.

    embrace (verb). 1. To clasp in the arms. 2. To enclose on all sides. 3. To take up readily or gladly. 4. To make use of.

    Which definition should the student use to understand the word "embraced" in the context of the sentence?

    (A) Definition 1
    (B) Definition 2
    (C) Definition 3
    (D) Definition 4

Questions 20–21 are based on the following passage, which students are reading in class.

One of the best-known blues guitarists might have faded into obscurity had it not been for an old atlas. In the late 1920's, the blues guitarist John Hurt made several recordings. Much later, in the 1960's, the folk music movement helped stir renewed interest in traditional American music. At that time, Tom Hoskins and Mike Stewart came across John Hurt's recording of "Avalon Blues." The guitar playing was so amazing that they tried to track down Hurt. They knew he was said to live in a Mississippi town named Avalon, but they could find no sign of him—or of the town of Avalon itself. Then they looked in an atlas from 1878. They found Avalon. John Hurt still lived there. The men made more recordings of Mississippi John Hurt, thus preserving his music for future generations.

20. The paraprofessional asks the students to identify the main purpose of the passage. Which response from the students is most accurate?

   (A) To explain where blues music began
   (B) To explain how Hurt was rediscovered
   (C) To discuss music created by Hoskins and Stewart
   (D) To explain how Hurt influenced later blues musicians

21. What question could the paraprofessional ask the students that would help them better understand the particular steps that Hoskins and Stewart took to find Hurt?

   (A) Why did Hoskins and Stewart need to look in an 1878 atlas?
   (B) Why were Hoskins and Stewart looking for Hurt?
   (C) What kind of music did Hurt record?
   (D) What kind of music was popular during the 1960's?

Questions 22–24 are based on the following excerpt adapted from a book that students are reading.

Amy Goes Fishing
Chapter 1: Worms

It was Saturday morning. Amy and her family were having breakfast.

Amy's brother, Bill, got up.

"Good-bye," he said with his mouth full of pancakes. "I'm going to a baseball game."

Then Amy's sister, Meg, got up.

"Good-bye," she said. "My Girl Scout meeting starts at ten."

Amy's mother pushed back her chair. "I have to work today," she said. "Good-bye, Amy. Good-bye, Dan. Don't forget to take out the garbage."

Amy wished she had a good place to go. *Clang!* She dropped her fork.

"What was that?" her dad asked. He looked at the empty chairs. "Everyone is gone except you and me," he said.

"What can we do?" Amy asked.

22. Students are learning to make predictions about a story by using clues from the title of the story, the chapter headings, and what happens in the story itself. The paraprofessional asks students what Amy and her father will most likely do next. Which response from the students shows the strongest understanding of the clues?

(A) Amy and her father will make pancakes together.
(B) Amy and her father will go to Bill's baseball game.
(C) Amy and her father will go fishing.
(D) Amy and her father will find jobs of their own.

23. Students have been given a mixed-up list of things that happen in the story. Here is the mixed-up list:

   I. Meg says good-bye.
   II. Amy asks her father what they should do.
   III. Amy's mother says good-bye.
   IV. Amy drops her fork.
   V. Bill says good-bye.

The students are asked to put the events in the order in which they happen in the story. What is the correct order?

(A) I, V, III, IV, II
(B) II, III, I, V, IV
(C) V, I, III, IV, II
(D) V, III, I, II, IV

24. Students are learning how to recognize and pronounce words that begin with *blended* consonant sounds, such as the word *frog,* which begins with the blending of /f/ and /r/ consonant sounds. Which word from the story is the clearest example of a word that begins with a blended consonant sound?

(A) baseball
(B) clang
(C) fork
(D) garbage

Questions 25–26 are based on the following passage, which students are reading in class.

Line

The telegraph, which was invented in 1837, allowed people to communicate almost instantly across long distances. It required a wire to carry the signal from
5 sender to recipient. The first telegraph lines could only be strung across poles overland. Since water would prevent a poorly insulated wire from functioning, underwater cables could not be laid until
10 a special cable was developed. The first underwater cable was laid between New York City and Fort Lee, New Jersey, in 1845. Six years later, an underwater cable from England to France created the first
15 international connection. Seven years after that, an underwater cable from New York to Ireland created the first transatlantic telegraph connection.

25. Students are learning about prefixes. The paraprofessional asks them to think of a word that contains the same prefix as "telegraph." Which student's word is correct?

(A) Motel
(B) Telephone
(C) Graphic
(D) Monograph

26. A paraprofessional is working with a student who is having trouble understanding the word "transatlantic" (line 17). What would be an effective strategy for the paraprofessional to use to help the student understand that word?

(A) Ask the student to write a sentence that contains the word "transatlantic."
(B) Using a map, point out that Ireland and New York are on different sides of the Atlantic Ocean.
(C) Point out to the student when the first underwater cable was developed.
(D) Have the student identify ways that people can communicate over long distances.

Questions 27–29 are based on the following lesson plan created by the teacher.

Lesson Plan for Working with Compound Words

Objective: Students will use their knowledge of the individual words that make up unknown compound words to determine the meanings of the unknown words.

Description: The teacher explains the concept of *compound words* (two separate words joined to form a new word) to the students. The paraprofessional passes out a handout made by the teacher that has four compound words on it: *sunbeam, sandbox, scarecrow, thumbprint.* Students draw a line between the two words that make up each compound word and then write down what they think each compound word means. Finally, students invent their own, "new" compound words by combining two words. The teacher and the paraprofessional help individual students with this task. The paraprofessional collects the papers and places them in alphabetical order by the students' last names.

27. The lesson plan indicates that the paraprofessional should do each of the following EXCEPT

    (A) distribute the handout
    (B) collect the handout
    (C) explain the concept of compound words
    (D) help students invent compound words

28. There are four students in the class whose last name starts with "A." How should their names be alphabetized?

    (A) Alvarez, Anderson, Ames, Ahmed
    (B) Alvarez, Ames, Ahmed, Anderson
    (C) Ahmed, Ames, Alvarez, Anderson
    (D) Ahmed, Alvarez, Ames, Anderson

29. Four students have written down words that they believe are "new" compound words. Which word indicates the strongest understanding of compound words?

    (A) teacherist
    (B) mousefood
    (C) pencilly
    (D) unbook

30. Students are thinking up pairs of words that are antonyms. Four students' pairs are printed below. Which is a pair of antonyms?

    (A) Bare and bear
    (B) Careless and cautious
    (C) Effort and attempt
    (D) Quiet and quit

MATHEMATICS

Directions for Questions 31– 60: Each of the questions or incomplete statements below is followed by four suggested answers or completions. Select the one that is best in each case and fill in the corresponding lettered space on the answer sheet with a heavy, dark mark so that you cannot see the letter.

31. $24 \times 16 =$

(A) 384
(B) 364
(C) 224
(D) 168

$$\frac{1}{6}, \frac{2}{7}, \frac{3}{4}, \frac{5}{8}$$

32. Which of the following is NOT the numerator of a fraction listed above?

(A) 2
(B) 3
(C) 4
(D) 5

33. For a class trip, it takes $1\frac{4}{5}$ hours to drive from Kennedy High School to the science museum. How many minutes long is the drive?

(A) 64 min
(B) 68 min
(C) 108 min
(D) 120 min

34. What is the shape of the sign shown above?

(A) Triangle
(B) Hexagon
(C) Octagon
(D) Rectangle

35. A class is doing an art project with pipe cleaners. The teacher has 120 pipe cleaners and there are 30 students in the class. If each student receives the same number of pipe cleaners, how many pipe cleaners does each student receive?

(A) 3
(B) 4
(C) 5
(D) 9

36. Which of the following is true?

(A) $3 + 4 < 7$
(B) $-5 > 0$
(C) $2 + 7 = 6 + 3$
(D) $-8 + 9 < 0$

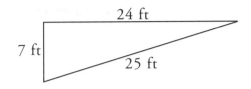

37. A class is designing a triangular garden as shown above. What is the perimeter of the garden?

    (A) 56 ft
    (B) 84 ft
    (C) 168 ft
    (D) 175 ft

38. $4^5 =$

    (A) 4×5
    (B) $4 \div 5$
    (C) $5 \times 5 \times 5 \times 5$
    (D) $4 \times 4 \times 4 \times 4 \times 4$

39. If $5k = 55$, what is the value of k?

    (A)   5
    (B)   11
    (C)   50
    (D) 275

| $10 | $1 | $1 | 25¢ | 25¢ |

40. Which of the following is NOT equivalent to the total amount of money represented above?

    (A) $12.50
    (B) 12.50¢
    (C) 1,250 cents
    (D) Twelve dollars and fifty cents

41. Of the 28 students in a class, 7 went on a band trip. What percent of the class went on the trip?

    (A) 35%
    (B) 25%
    (C) 7%
    (D) 4%

RECIPE	
Ingredients	*Amount*
Sugar	One-half of a cup
Flour	Two-thirds of a cup
Chocolate	Three-eighths of a cup
Baking powder	Five-eighths of a cup
Milk	Seven-eighths of a cup

42. A partial list of ingredients for a recipe is shown above. For how many of the ingredients is the amount listed less than $\frac{3}{4}$ cup?

    (A) Two
    (B) Three
    (C) Four
    (D) Five

43. 327.65

If the ones digit and the hundredths digit were interchanged in the number above, which of the following would be the resulting number?

(A) 723.65
(B) 627.35
(C) 527.63
(D) 325.67

44. 1, 2, 3, 5, 8, …

Starting with the third term in the sequence above, each term is the sum of the two preceding terms. If this pattern is continued, what will be the sixth term in the sequence?

(A) 12
(B) 13
(C) 14
(D) 21

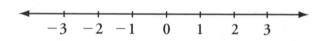

45. On the number line above, the number -1.3 is located between which two numbers?

(A) -3 and -2
(B) -2 and -1
(C) -1 and 0
(D) 0 and 1

46. Which of the following is equivalent to 3%?

(A) $\dfrac{3}{10}$

(B) $\dfrac{100}{3}$

(C) 3

(D) 0.03

Week	Height (inches)
1	0.25
2	0.50
3	0.75
4	1.00
⋮	⋮

47. The table above shows the height of a plant at the end of each week. The height increases by the same amount each week. If this pattern continues, what will be the height, in inches, of the plant at the end of the 7th week?

(A) 1.25 in
(B) 1.50 in
(C) 1.75 in
(D) 2.00 in

$$16 = \boxed{}^{2}$$
What number should be placed in the box to solve the problem?

---

48. A student is not sure how to answer the problem shown above. Which of the following questions could Mr. Jennings ask the student in order to provide help?

    (A) What number multiplied by itself equals 16?
    (B) What is the result if 16 is multiplied by itself?
    (C) What is the result if 16 is multiplied by 2?
    (D) What number multiplied by 2 equals 16?

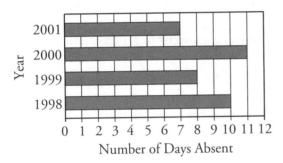
Number of Days Absent

49. The graph above shows the number of days that Tom was absent from school for each of four years. For the four years shown, the total number of days Tom was absent was

    (A) fewer than 32 days
    (B) between 32 and 38 days
    (C) between 38 and 44 days
    (D) more than 44 days

50. $197.38 + 6.7 =$

    (A) 198.05
    (B) 204.08
    (C) 264.38
    (D) 867.38

51. During November, a ninth-grade class collected 18 pounds 14 ounces of aluminum cans to be recycled, and a tenth-grade class collected 22 pounds 1 ounce of aluminum cans. How many more ounces of cans did the tenth-grade class collect than the ninth-grade class?

    (A) 43 oz
    (B) 45 oz
    (C) 51 oz
    (D) 67 oz

52. $\dfrac{199.17}{401.05}$ is approximately equal to

    (A) 0.25
    (B) 0.5
    (C) 2
    (D) 4

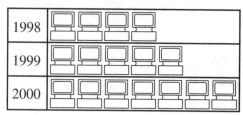

1998	
1999	
2000	

Each 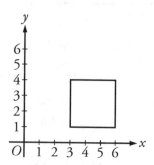 represents 5 computers

53. The graph above shows the number of computers a certain elementary school had for each of three years. How many more computers did the school have in 2000 than in 1998?

(A) 30
(B) 15
(C) 5
(D) 3

$$\text{Equation:} \quad 5x = 100$$
$$\text{Solution:} \quad x = 20$$

54. An equation and its solution are shown above. Ms. Lee helps a student to check the solution. Which of the following is a correct explanation?

(A) Replace the x in the equation with 20, multiply by 5, and check to see if the left and right sides of the equation are equal.
(B) Replace the x in the equation with 20, add 5, and check to see if the left and right sides of the equation are equal.
(C) Replace the x in the equation with 20, divide by 5, and check to see if the left and right sides of the equation are equal.
(D) Replace the x in the equation with 20, subtract 5, and check to see if the left and right sides of the equation are equal.

55. In the xy-plane above, which of the following points is NOT inside the square?

(A) (5,2)
(B) (4.5,2.5)
(C) (4,3)
(D) (2,5)

56. For second period, $\frac{2}{5}$ of the students in Mrs. Brown's class went to art class and $\frac{1}{3}$ went to music class. What fraction of the number of students went to either art or music class?

(A) $\frac{3}{8}$

(B) $\frac{11}{15}$

(C) $\frac{5}{6}$

(D) $\frac{6}{5}$

57. Diana is grading a student's project. The student's project score is 80, but the student earned a 5% bonus of the project score by doing an extra-credit assignment. Which of the following is a correct procedure that Diana can use to calculate the student's score, including the bonus?

(A) $80 + 0.05 \times 80$
(B) 80×0.05
(C) $80 + 0.05$
(D) $80 + 5$

58. Which of the following shows the numbers from least to greatest?

(A) $\frac{1}{4}, \frac{3}{10}, \frac{1}{8}$

(B) $\frac{1}{8}, \frac{1}{4}, \frac{3}{10}$

(C) $\frac{1}{8}, \frac{3}{10}, \frac{1}{4}$

(D) $\frac{3}{10}, \frac{1}{8}, \frac{1}{4}$

$$5 - 3 + 2 + 2 \times 4 =$$

59. Juan helps a student to solve the problem above. Which of the following is the first operation that Juan should instruct the student to do?

(A) $5 - 3$
(B) $3 + 2$
(C) $2 + 2$
(D) 2×4

60. Susan scored an 84 and an 88 on 2 tests. What is the average (arithmetic mean) of these 2 test scores?

(A) 82
(B) 84
(C) 86
(D) 88

WRITING

Directions for Questions 61–68: In each of the sentences below, four portions are underlined and lettered. Read each sentence and select the underlined portion that contains a grammatical construction, a word use, or an instance of punctuation that would be inappropriate in carefully written English. Note the letter printed beneath the underlined portion you select and completely fill in the corresponding lettered space on the answer sheet with a heavy, dark mark so that you cannot see the letter. <u>No sentence has more than one error.</u>

Example:

Margaret <u>insist</u> <u>that</u> the hat <u>,</u> coat, and
      A   B   C

<u>scarf</u> are hers.
 D

Sample Answer:

61. A recent documentary <u>examines</u> several early
                       A

radio <u>broadcast</u> by African American disk
       B

jockeys, <u>as well as</u> their struggle <u>to achieve</u>
        C   D

station ownership.

62. Strawberries <u>are</u> expensive <u>to grow</u> , but
            A   B

<u>they</u> can yield more profits per acre <u>then</u>
 C   D

almost any other crop.

63. Women pilots, from Amelia Earhart <u>to</u>
                              A

contemporary pilot Doris Lockness <u>;</u>
                            B

<u>have been flying</u> <u>since</u> 1908.
      C   D

64. <u>Most</u> cities and towns in the United States
    A

have ordinances <u>regulating</u> the height of any
               B

fence <u>built</u> within <u>its</u> borders.
      C   D

65. The common housefly <u>breeds</u> more
                          A

    <u>frequent</u> when humidity <u>is</u> low and
      B   C

    temperatures are <u>warm</u> .
                       D

66. In the mid-nineteenth century, the name

    "Jack" became popular <u>as</u> an English first
                            A

    name, <u>and</u> it <u>remains</u> so until its use
            B   C

    declined <u>after peaking</u> in the 1920's.
                  D

67. Scientists <u>are discovering</u> increasing
                      A

    <u>evidence that</u> flavonoids <u>,</u> a group of
          B   C

    chemicals found in certain plant species,

    <u>has</u> a beneficial effect on human health.
     D

68. The mountain <u>known as</u> Irazu, located
                     A

    <u>near</u> the capital of Costa Rica, <u>is</u> one of
      B   C

    the <u>countries</u> most active volcanoes.
          D

Directions for Questions 69–90: Each of the questions or incomplete statements below is followed by four suggested answers or completions. Select the one that is best in each case and fill in the corresponding lettered space on the answer sheet with a heavy, dark mark so that you cannot see the letter.

69. Diverse and hardy plants, palms grow in African streams, 9,000-foot-high Andean mountainsides, sweltering Southeast Asian swamps, and blizzard-lashed Himalayan highlands.

    What is the <u>subject</u> of the sentence above?

    (A) palms
    (B) streams
    (C) mountainsides
    (D) highlands

70. Many bicyclists used goggles and other specialized sports clothing during the bicycling craze that occurred in the United States in the 1890's.

    What is the <u>simple predicate</u> (the verb that tells what the subject does) in the sentence above?

    (A) used
    (B) during
    (C) bicycling
    (D) occurred

71. The educational vision of innovative Italian educator Maria Montessori is thriving as never before, with some 5,000 Montessori schools in the United States alone.

What is the <u>subject</u> of the sentence above?

(A) vision
(B) educator
(C) Maria Montessori
(D) schools

72. For over 50 years, Andrew Wyeth's spare and bright paintings of rural Pennsylvania and coastal Maine have attracted an enormous public following, even as art critics have <u>routinely</u> condemned his work.

In the sentence above, the underlined word is being used as

(A) a verb
(B) an adjective
(C) an adverb
(D) a preposition

73. The three greatest <u>threats</u> to the survival of the sage grouse, a bird that has long been native to North America, are range fires, farming, and livestock grazing.

In the sentence above, the underlined word is being used as

(A) a noun
(B) a verb
(C) an adjective
(D) an adverb

74. Some cities have banned the use of salt to treat icy roads, citing its tendency to corrode vehicles, pavement, bridges, and any unprotected steel <u>in</u> nearby structures.

In the sentence above, the underlined word is being used as

(A) a verb
(B) a pronoun
(C) an adverb
(D) a preposition

75. Which word is NOT spelled correctly?

(A) image
(B) privilege
(C) religion
(D) villege

76. Which word is NOT spelled correctly?

(A) reasonible
(B) receive
(C) recognize
(D) resolve

77. Which word is NOT spelled correctly?

(A) garage
(B) muscle
(C) preamble
(D) practicle

78. Which word is NOT spelled correctly?

(A) accomplish
(B) apparent
(C) dillema
(D) disappoint

79. Carl is writing a paper about the cellist Yo-Yo Ma. He wants to find out the date and place of Yo-Yo Ma's birth. What would be the best source for Carl to use to find this information quickly?

(A) A newspaper article about the origins of the cello
(B) An encyclopedia entry for Yo-Yo Ma
(C) A book about famous musicians
(D) An Internet review of Yo-Yo Ma's latest work

Questions 80–81 are based on the following rough draft written by a student.

How Many Friends is Enough?
by Pedro, Grade 5

(1) Some people think it's a good idea to have one very close friend, but I think it's best to have lots of friends. (2) If you have a lot of friends, you get to know many different kinds of people. (3) This can help you throughout your life. (4) Some things are more fun to do with a group of friends. (5) Some things I can think of are going to a ball game or having a party. (6) I can understand why some people take the other point of view and want just one close friend. (7) If you have just one close friend, you have more time to understand how another person thinks. (8) Secrets that you share with just one friend have a better chance of staying secret.

80. Pedro's teacher has instructed Pedro to divide his essay into two paragraphs, one paragraph for each main idea in the essay. Which sentence should be the opening sentence of the second paragraph?

(A) Sentence 3
(B) Sentence 4
(C) Sentence 6
(D) Sentence 7

81. Pedro wants to make his essay more persuasive by adding supporting arguments. Which sentence could Pedro add to his essay as an argument to support the point that it is best to have a lot of friends?

(A) Having a lot of friends means you will learn more news about what's going on in your neighborhood.
(B) People who have a lot of friends spend too much time trying to get them all to like each other.
(C) People should spend less time hanging out with their friends and spend more time with their families.
(D) If you have a lot of friends and you move away, it will be very tiring to keep in touch with all of them.

Questions 82–84 are based on the following unfinished outline.

Denise is writing an article for her school newspaper about the books that students in her middle school like to read. To research her article, she has spoken with the school librarian and with many students. Before writing, Denise must organize her research notes into an outline.

Kinds of Books That People My Age Like

I. Exciting Books
    A. Adventure Books
        1. Wizards and dragons
        2. Wild places
        3. Robots and aliens
    B. Mystery Books
        1. _____
        2. Strange but true events

II. _____
    A. Funny Stories
        1. Humor in fictional situations
        2. Funny things that happened to famous people
    B. Joke Books
        1. Collections of jokes
        2. Remarks by comedians

III. Books About Growing Up
    A. Fiction
        1. Problems with family
        2. Problems with friends and school
    B. Nonfiction
        1. Biographies
        2. Advice books

82. Denise has left heading I.B.1 (underneath "Mystery Books") blank. She goes back to her research notes to see what she should put into the blank to complete the section. Which of the headings below best fits in the blank?

(A) Science and technology encyclopedias
(B) Collections of riddles and puzzles
(C) Detective fiction
(D) Travel stories

83. What should Denise put in the blank for heading II as a title for the section?

(A) Amusing Characters
(B) Easy-to-read Books
(C) Limericks and Nonsense Rhymes
(D) Humorous Books

84. After Denise has completed her outline, she writes several drafts of the first sentence for her article. She wants to strike the right tone for her intended audience. Which of the following sentences is most appropriate in tone and language for publication in a school newspaper?

(A) I wish the geniuses who buy the books for the library would stop buying such awful stuff.
(B) Middle school students find certain kinds of books especially enjoyable.
(C) Some people waste their time watching hours of television when they should be reading.
(D) Middle school students like many kinds of books, but many of them are worthless junk.

Questions 85–87 are based on the following rough draft written by a student.

How to Buy Apples at the Supermarket
by Alexander, Grade 5

(1) Choose a kind of apple that you enjoy eating. (2) Some apples look good but don't have much flavor. (3) I really like Granny Smith apples. (4) Don't just choose the cheapest kind, sometimes a low price just means that the apples are getting old. (5) Each time you pick up an apple, look at it carefully. (6) Be sure it doesn't have any soft spots. (7) Look out for dents or insect damage. (8) Put the apple in your bag carefully. (9) Don't buy too many, or some will get old before you eat them.

85. Alexander wants his essay to begin with a sentence that introduces the central point he is trying to make. Which sentence would best introduce Alexander's central point?

(A) Everyone should eat fruit, and apples are a good food to have as part of your diet.
(B) Supermarkets sometimes sell fruit that you wouldn't want to find on your table.
(C) If you want to bring home good and tasty apples, choose them carefully.
(D) My favorite part of the supermarket is where they keep the fresh fruit.

86. Alexander wants to combine sentences 6 and 7 so that they form a single sentence that is clear, concise, and grammatically correct. What would be the most effective revision for sentences 6 and 7?

(A) Be sure it doesn't have any soft spots, look out for dents or insect damage.
(B) Be sure it doesn't have any soft spots, dents, or insect damage.
(C) Be sure it doesn't have any soft spots, or does it have either dents or insect damage.
(D) Be sure it doesn't have any soft spots, and dents and insect damage, too.

87. Alexander is learning how to use transition words (words that clarify the relationships between ideas). What transition word or words should Alexander use before the word "sometimes" in sentence 4 in order to clarify the meaning of the sentence?

(A) but
(B) because
(C) for example,
(D) so

Question 88–89 refer to the following classroom situation.

Students are learning how to write essays for different purposes, such as to compare, to instruct, to persuade, or to describe. They have been instructed to choose a primary purpose for their essay and then write an introductory sentence for the essay that clearly conveys that purpose. Four students' sentences are printed below.

I. My skateboard is designed to roll like a racing car and fly like a jet plane.

II. Our school must offer more courses about real-life skills, such as how to find a job, and it must do so immediately.

III. Making a sock puppet is easy and requires just one old sock and a lot of imagination.

IV. My favorite movie and my favorite television show have a lot of things in common.

88. Which introductory sentence most strongly suggests that the primary purpose of the essay is to explore a comparison?

(A) Sentence I
(B) Sentence II
(C) Sentence III
(D) Sentence IV

89. Which introductory sentence most strongly suggests that the primary purpose of the essay is to persuade?

(A) Sentence I
(B) Sentence II
(C) Sentence III
(D) Sentence IV

90. Students are learning the general rule to follow when forming the plural of nouns that end in *-y* preceded by a consonant (such as *fly* and *dictionary*). What is the rule?

(A) Add *-s* to the end of the noun.
(B) Add *-'s* to the end of the noun.
(C) Double the consonant and then add *-es*.
(D) Change the *-y* to *-i* and then add *-es*.

Chapter 8
Right Answers and Explanations for the Practice Test

▶ ▶ ▶ ▶ ▶ ▶ ▶ ▶ ▶ ▶ ▶ ▶

Right Answers and Explanations for the Practice Test

Now that you have answered all of the practice questions, you can check your work. Compare your answers with the correct answers in the table below. You can also see the content category for each question. Then turn the page to find explanations for each question.

Question Number	Correct Answer	Content Category
1	D	Reading Skills: Main idea/primary purpose
2	A	Reading Skills: Inferences
3	D	Reading Skills: Main idea/primary purpose
4	C	Reading Skills: Supporting ideas
5	B	Reading Skills: Main idea/primary purpose
6	D	Reading Skills: Vocabulary in context
7	B	Reading Skills: Inferences
8	A	Reading Skills: Inferences
9	D	Reading Skills: Supporting ideas
10	A	Reading Skills: Supporting ideas
11	B	Reading Skills: Organization
12	C	Reading Skills: Interpreting graphic text
13	D	Reading Skills: Organization
14	B	Reading Skills: Supporting ideas
15	D	Reading Skills: Main idea/primary purpose
16	D	Reading Skills: Fact/opinion
17	C	Reading Skills: Interpreting graphic text
18	A	Reading Skills: Interpreting graphic text
19	C	Reading Application: Using a dictionary
20	B	Reading Application: Making accurate observations
21	A	Reading Application: Asking questions
22	C	Reading Application: Prereading strategies
23	C	Reading Application: Making accurate observations
24	B	Reading Application: Sounding out words
25	B	Reading Application: Breaking down words into parts
26	B	Reading Application: Decoding words using context clues
27	C	Reading Application: Interpreting directions
28	D	Reading Application: Alphabetizing words
29	B	Reading Application: Breaking down words into parts
30	B	Reading Application: Synonyms, antonyms, and homonyms
31	A	Math Skills: Number Sense and Basic Algebra
32	C	Math Skills: Number Sense and Basic Algebra
33	C	Math Application: Geometry and Measurement
34	C	Math Skills: Geometry and Measurement
35	B	Math Application: Number Sense and Basic Algebra
36	C	Math Skills: Number Sense and Basic Algebra
37	A	Math Application: Geometry and Measurement
38	D	Math Skills: Number Sense and Basic Algebra
39	B	Math Skills: Number Sense and Basic Algebra
40	B	Math Skills: Geometry and Measurement
41	B	Math Application: Number Sense and Basic Algebra
42	C	Math Skills: Number Sense and Basic Algebra
43	D	Math Skills: Number Sense and Basic Algebra
44	B	Math Skills: Number Sense and Basic Algebra
45	B	Math Skills: Number Sense and Basic Algebra

Question Number	Correct Answer	Content Category
46	D	Math Skills: Number Sense and Basic Algebra
47	C	Math Skills: Data Analysis
48	A	Math Application: Number Sense and Basic Algebra
49	B	Math Application: Data Analysis
50	B	Math Skills: Number Sense and Basic Algebra
51	C	Math Application: Geometry and Measurement
52	B	Math Skills: Number Sense and Basic Algebra
53	B	Math Application: Data Analysis
54	A	Math Application: Number Sense and Basic Algebra
55	D	Math Skills: Geometry and Measurement
56	B	Math Application: Number Sense and Basic Algebra
57	A	Math Application: Number Sense and Basic Algebra
58	B	Math Skills: Number Sense and Basic Algebra
59	D	Math Application: Number Sense and Basic Algebra
60	C	Math Application: Data Analysis
61	B	Writing Skills: Grammatical errors
62	D	Writing Skills: Errors in word usage
63	B	Writing Skills: Errors in punctuation
64	D	Writing Skills: Grammatical errors
65	B	Writing Skills: Grammatical errors
66	C	Writing Skills: Grammatical errors
67	D	Writing Skills: Grammatical errors
68	D	Writing Skills: Errors in punctuation
69	A	Writing Skills: Parts of a sentence
70	A	Writing Skills: Parts of a sentence
71	A	Writing Skills: Parts of a sentence
72	C	Writing Skills: Parts of speech
73	A	Writing Skills: Parts of speech
74	D	Writing Skills: Parts of speech
75	D	Writing Skills: Spelling
76	A	Writing Skills: Spelling
77	D	Writing Skills: Spelling
78	C	Writing Skills: Spelling
79	B	Writing Application: Reference materials
80	C	Writing Application: Drafting and revising
81	A	Writing Application: Writing in different modes and forms
82	C	Writing Application: Prewriting
83	D	Writing Application: Prewriting
84	B	Writing Application: Writing for different purposes and audiences
85	C	Writing Application: Drafting and revising
86	B	Writing Application: Editing written documents
87	B	Writing Application: Editing written documents
88	D	Writing Application: Writing in different modes and forms
89	B	Writing Application: Writing in different modes and forms
90	D	Writing Application: Editing written documents

Explanations of Right Answers

READING

1. The correct answer is (D). The passage mentions the colony established by a group of English people in 1620 and then points out that that colony was one of many that had already been established around the world by Europeans at that time. (A) and (B) are incorrect because they refer to specific information about the daily life and government of the colonies that is not offered in the passage. (C) is incorrect because it refers to a broader topic—the development of trade routes between Europe and the United States—than the one discussed in the passage.

2. The correct answer is (A). The passage states that the ocelot population in Texas has declined because of loss of its habitat. The passage goes on to state that a large percentage of the native land cover of Texas has been altered and that the ocelot has been unable to adapt to the decrease in the thick vegetation that gives it protection. Thus, it can be inferred that the change that caused the decline in the ocelot population was loss of thick vegetation and that the ocelot needs a habitat that provides a lot of land cover.

3. The correct answer is (D). In the excerpt, the narrator describes playing in a frozen puddle with Cathy while the twins from next door are playing on a tire swing.

4. The correct answer is (C). The narrator (the character who is telling the story) says she thought that the cracked ice in the puddle looked like "the crystal paperweight Granny kept in the parlor." (B) is not correct because it was Cathy rather than the narrator who thought the frozen puddle looked like a spider web.

5. The correct answer is (B). The passage opens by stating that, until the 1970's, most literature published by Native American women was poetry. It then goes on to mention the different kinds of literature published by Native American women more recently: the novels written by Hale and Silko, and the work combining poetry and prose written by Cook. The works of these three authors represent developments in literature published by Native Americans. (A) and (C) are incorrect because the passage does not focus on a particular novel, a particular theory, or a particular author. (D) is incorrect because, although the passage does mention the works of three different authors, it does so in order to point out one of their similarities.

6. The correct answer is (D). In the passage, the word "body" is used to refer to the entire group of works that make up Native American literature written by women. The author's point is that Hale, Silko, and Cook have added something new to this collection.

7. The correct answer is (B). The passage states that Hale, Silko, and Cook are publishing literature that differs from the literature previously published by Native American women, in the sense that these writers "no longer express themselves exclusively in traditional forms" (lines 13–14). Thus, the three women authors are "helping to reshape Native American literature."

8. The correct answer is (A). The first paragraph indicates how central water travel was to the Egyptians. The second paragraph describes a puzzle connected to two particular ships: archaeologists do not understand why these ships were so large or why they were buried at King Khufu's gravesite. Thus, the passage indicates that, although water travel was important to the Egyptians, archaeologists do not completely understand all aspects of the Egyptians' relationship to ships.

9. The correct answer is (D). The first sentence of the second paragraph states that the two 4,600-year-old ships "are huge in comparison to other Egyptian ships" (lines 18–19). (C) is incorrect because the first sentence of the second paragraph establishes that the two ships were made of wood.

10. The correct answer is (A). The second sentence of the first paragraph states that because water travel was important to Egyptians, "they liked to display drawings of ships in their tombs" (lines 6–7). (C) is incorrect because the second paragraph indicates that Egyptians did place miniature ships in their tombs.

11. The correct answer is (B). Toward the end of the second paragraph, the author mentions that one theory about the ships' purpose was that they were used to transport King Khufu's body to his gravesite. In the following sentence, the author mentions that marks on the ships' wood may indicate that the ships were once in water and in motion; the mention of the marks provides possible support for the theory about the ships' purpose. (A) is incorrect because the water marks are mentioned in the context of a discussion about why the Egyptians buried the 4,600-year-old ships in King Khufu's tomb. (C) is incorrect because the marks are not mentioned in connection with the first theory discussed in the second paragraph, which is that the ships were buried for Khufu's use in the afterlife. (D) is incorrect because, although the passage does present one theory to explain why the ships were taken apart, the marks on the wood are not mentioned in order to explain this theory. Instead, they are mentioned specifically as evidence that the ships had once been in water.

12. The correct answer is (C). The graph shows that about 14 reptile species are considered endangered. (A) and (D) are incorrect because the graph does not provide any information about the reasons species are becoming endangered. (B) is incorrect because the graph does not provide any information about different regions of the United States.

13. The correct answer is (D). The second paragraph opens with a general statement about giant kelp: it has a "major effect on the ocean and sea creatures around it." The paragraph then goes on to list specific ways in which the giant kelp affects the ocean: providing food, shelter, shade, and safety for sea creatures, and softening the action of ocean waves. Thus, the general statement about giant kelp is supported with these specific examples of evidence. (A), (B), and (C) are incorrect because the passage does not describe a problem, present an argument, or discuss an event.

14. The correct answer is (B). The question asks for a characteristic of giant kelp that is NOT mentioned in the passage. (B) refers to the use of kelp as a possible food source for humans, and the passage does NOT mention this idea. Each of the other concepts is mentioned in the passage. (A) is mentioned in the first sentence. (C) and (D) are both mentioned in the second paragraph.

15. The correct answer is (D). The passage describes the author setting out on a trip and mentions the places to which he will travel. (A) and (B) are incorrect because the author neither discusses his childhood nor makes a statement about the effects of travel. (C) is incorrect because, although the author does discuss mapmakers and small towns, these topics are not the central focus of the passage.

16. The correct answer is (D). The first three sentences present facts about the practice of basing early movies on children's books. The last sentence expresses the author's opinion about the appropriateness of that practice.

17. The correct answer is (C). Chapter 1 is organized by geographical region during the colonial period: New England, the Middle Colonies, the South. The table of contents as a whole is organized by time period, but the question asks only how chapter 1 is organized.

18. The correct answer is (A). The period around 1765 is discussed in Chapter 2: THE FORMING OF THE REPUBLIC (1760–1820). Within this chapter, the section entitled, "Fiction, Poetry, and Drama," which starts on page 43, can be expected to discuss fiction.

19. The correct answer is (C). In the sentence, "embraced" is being used to indicate that Maria eagerly took up the cause of environmental justice after the bay near her home became polluted.

20. The correct answer is (B). The passage focuses on discussing Hoskins and Stewart's interest in Hurt's music and the process they went through to find him. Thus the passage primarily describes how Hurt was rediscovered. (A) is incorrect because the passage discusses only one particular blues musician, not where blues as a musical style began. (C) is incorrect because Hoskins and Stewart are discussed only in relation to Hurt; no information is offered about whether they are musicians. (D) is incorrect because the passage focuses on finding Hurt and not on ways he might have influenced later musicians.

21. The correct answer is (A). Only the question asked in (A) would help students think about the specific process that Hoskins and Stewart used to look for Hurt because (A) draws students' attention to the use of the 1878

atlas, which is what ultimately allowed Hoskins and Stewart to locate Hurt. (B), (C), and (D) are incorrect because, in answering those questions, students would be led away from how Hoskins and Stewart found Hurt.

22. The correct answer is (C). In the story, Amy's sister, brother, and mother leave breakfast to go to various activities; Amy and her father are alone at home with nothing to do. The title of the book the students are reading is *Amy Goes Fishing,* and the chapter heading is "Worms." Thus, the clues suggest that Amy and her father will go fishing. (A) is incorrect because Amy and her father are just finishing breakfast in the story. (B) is incorrect because only Bill is described in the story as preparing to go to a baseball game.

23. The correct answer is (C). First Bill says good-bye, then Meg, and then Amy's mother. Amy wishes she had someplace to go, drops her fork, and asks her father what they can do.

24. The correct answer is (B). The word begins with the blending of the consonants /c/ and /l/.

25. The correct answer is (B). Both "telegraph" and "telephone" have the prefix "tele."

26. The correct answer is (B). By pointing out New York and Ireland on a map, the paraprofessional can explain that transatlantic means that the underwater cable crossed the Atlantic Ocean. (A) is incorrect because if the student does not understand the word "transatlantic," he or she is unlikely to be able to use it in a sentence. (C) is incorrect because

the date of the development of the first underwater cable is not clearly relevant to the meaning of "transatlantic." (D) is incorrect because it shifts the student's attention away from the meaning of "transatlantic" to words that describe methods of communicating, and these kinds of words are not directly connected to the meaning of "transatlantic."

27. The correct answer is (C). The second sentence indicates that the paraprofessional should pass out the handout (A). The last sentence indicates that the paraprofessional should collect the handout (B). The fifth sentence indicates that both the teacher and paraprofessional will help students invent compound words (D). The first sentence indicates that the teacher, NOT the paraprofessional, will explain the concept of compound words.

28. The correct answer is (D). All the names begin with "A," so they have to be alphabetized on the basis of each name's second letter.

29. The correct answer is (B). "Mousefood" is a combination of the separate words "mouse" and "food" and is therefore a compound word. None of the other options contains two separate words put together. Instead, (A) and (C) each contain a word and a suffix, and (D) contains a prefix and a word.

30. The correct answer is (B). Antonyms are words that are opposite in meaning: "careless" and "cautious" are opposites. None of the other word pairs are opposites.

MATH

31. Rewrite the multiplication problem as follows:

$$\begin{array}{r} 24 \\ \times 16 \end{array}$$

Then calculate using partial products.

$$\begin{array}{r} 24 \\ \times 16 \\ \hline 144 \\ 24 \\ \hline 384 \end{array}$$

Therefore, the correct answer is (A), 384.

32. In a fraction, the number on the top is the numerator and the number on bottom is the denominator. Thus, for the fractions

$$\frac{1}{6}, \frac{2}{7}, \frac{3}{4}, \text{ and } \frac{5}{8}$$

the numerators are 1, 2, 3, and 5. Therefore, of the answer choices given, 4 is the only number that is NOT a numerator, and (C) is therefore the correct answer.

33. 1 hour is equivalent to 60 minutes. To convert $\frac{4}{5}$ hour to minutes, multiply $\frac{4}{5}$ by 60:

$$\frac{4}{5} \times 60 = 48$$

To find the length of the drive, add the number of minutes in 1 hour and the number of minutes in $\frac{4}{5}$ of an hour.

60 minutes + 48 minutes = 108 minutes

Therefore, the correct answer is (C), 108 min.

34. The sign is a polygon, and in order to determine the shape of the sign, count the number of sides. Since the sign has eight sides, it is an octagon. Therefore, the correct answer is (C), octagon.

35. To determine the number of pipe cleaners each student received, divide the total number of pipe cleaners by the number of students.

total number of pipe cleaners ÷
total number of students =
number of pipe cleaners each student received

Since there are a total of 120 pipe cleaners and 30 students,

$$120 \div 30 = 4$$

Therefore, the correct answer is (B); each student received 4 pipe cleaners.

36. To determine which is true, examine each answer choice.

    $3 + 4 < 7$ is not true because $3 + 4$ is equal to 7, not less than 7.

    $-5 > 0$ is not true because -5 is a negative number and negative numbers are less than 0.

    $2 + 7 = 6 + 3$ is true because $2 + 7$ equals 9 and $6 + 3$ equals 9.

    $-8 + 9 < 0$ is not true because $-8 + 9$ is equal to 1, and 1 is greater than 0.

    Therefore, the correct answer is (C), $2 + 7 = 6 + 3$.

37. The perimeter of a triangle is the sum of the lengths of the sides of a triangle. To determine the perimeter of the triangular garden, add the lengths of the sides of the garden.

    $$7 \text{ ft} + 24 \text{ ft} + 25 \text{ ft} = 56 \text{ ft}$$

    Therefore, the correct answer is (A); the perimeter of the triangular garden is 56 ft.

38. In the expression 4^5, the exponent 5 represents the number of 4's multiplied together as follows:

    $$4^5 = 4 \times 4 \times 4 \times 4 \times 4$$

    Therefore, the correct answer is (D), $4 \times 4 \times 4 \times 4 \times 4$.

39. Since $5k = 55$, dividing both sides of the equation by 5 gives $\dfrac{5k}{5} = \dfrac{55}{5}$, and $k = 11$.

    Therefore, the correct answer is (B); value of k is 11.

40. First add $\$10 + \$1 + \$1 = \$12$

    Then add $25\cent + 25\cent = 50\cent = \$0.50$

    Thus the total amount of money is $12.50, or twelve dollars and fifty cents, which is 1,250 cents, not $12.50\cent$.

    Therefore, the correct answer is (B), $12.50\cent$.

41. To determine the percent of the class that went on the trip, first divide the number of students in the class that went on the band trip by the total number of students in the class. Since 7 students in the class went on the band trip and there are 28 students in the class:

    number of students in the class that went on the band trip ÷ total number of students in the class = $7 \div 28 = 0.25$

    In order to convert 0.25 to a percent, multiply 0.25 by 100:

    $$0.25 \times 100 = 25\%$$

    Therefore, the correct answer is (B), 25%.

42. For each ingredient in the recipe, compare the amount in the table with $\frac{3}{4}$ cup by cross multiplying:

Sugar: cross multiply $\frac{1}{2}$ and $\frac{3}{4}$; since $4 < 6$, $\frac{1}{2}$ is less than $\frac{3}{4}$.

Flour: cross multiply $\frac{2}{3}$ and $\frac{3}{4}$; since $8 < 9$, $\frac{2}{3}$ is less than $\frac{3}{4}$.

Chocolate: cross multiply $\frac{3}{8}$ and $\frac{3}{4}$; since $12 < 24$, $\frac{3}{8}$ is less than $\frac{3}{4}$.

Baking powder: cross multiply $\frac{5}{8}$ and $\frac{3}{4}$; since $20 < 24$, $\frac{5}{8}$ is less than $\frac{3}{4}$.

Milk: cross multiply $\frac{7}{8}$ and $\frac{3}{4}$; since $28 > 24$, $\frac{7}{8}$ is greater than $\frac{3}{4}$.

Therefore, the correct answer is (C). Four of the ingredients listed have amounts less than $\frac{3}{4}$ cup.

43. The ones digit is one place to the left of the decimal point, and the hundredths digit is two places to the right of the decimal point, as shown below.

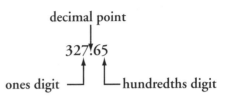

If the ones digit, 7, is replaced by the hundredths digit, 5, and the hundredths digit, 5, is replaced by the ones digit, 7, the result is

325.67

Therefore, the correct answer is (D), 325.67.

44. The sixth number in the sequence is equal to the sum of the fourth and fifth numbers in the sequence. Since the fourth number is 5 and the fifth number is 8, the sixth number is equal to $5+8=13$.

Therefore, the correct answer is (B), 13.

45. On the number line, a negative number is located to the left of 0. Since -1.3 is a negative number, it is located 1.3 units to the left of 0, which is between -2 and -1.

Therefore, the correct answer is (B); -1.3 is between -2 and -1.

46. To determine what is equivalent to 3%, convert 3% to a decimal by dividing 3 by 100.

$$\frac{3}{100} \text{ equals } 0.03.$$

Therefore, the correct answer is (D), 0.03.

47. To determine the plant's weekly change in height, choose any two consecutive weeks and subtract the earlier week's height from the later week's height. For example, if week 1 and week 2 are used, the weekly change in height can be determined as follows:

height at end of week 2 − height at end of week 1 = weekly change = 0.50 in. − 0.25 in. = 0.25 in.

For each week after the 4th week, add 0.25 in. to the height at the end of the previous week.

4th week = 1.00 in.
5th week = 1.00 in. + 0.25 in. = 1.25 in.
6th week = 1.25 in. + 0.25 in. = 1.50 in.
7th week = 1.50 in. + 0.25 in. = 1.75 in.

Therefore, the correct answer is (C); the height of the plant at the end of the 7th week is 1.75 in.

48. To help the student, Mr. Jennings needs to explain what $\square^2$ means.

The exponent, 2, means that the number in the box is multiplied by itself.

Therefore, the correct answer is (A). A helpful question is, "What number multiplied by itself equals 16?"

49. The length of each bar in the graph represents the number of days Tom was absent during a school year. According to the graph, in 1998 Tom was absent 10 days, in 1999 he was absent 8 days, in 2000 he was absent 11 days, and in 2001 he was absent 7 days. The total for the four years can be determined by adding the number of days Tom was absent each year.

10 days + 8 days + 11 days + 7 days = 36 days

Therefore, the correct answer is (B); Tom was absent a total of 36 days, which is between 32 and 38 days.

50. Rewrite the addition problem by lining up the decimal points as follows:

$$\begin{array}{r} 197.38 \\ + 6.70 \\ \hline \end{array}$$

Note that 6.70 is equivalent to 6.7.

Then calculate:

$$\begin{array}{r} {\scriptstyle 1\ 1\ 1} \\ 197.38 \\ + 6.70 \\ \hline 204.08 \end{array}$$

Therefore, the correct answer is (B), 204.08.

51. To determine how many more ounces of cans the tenth-grade class collected than the ninth-grade class, subtract the weight of cans collected by the ninth-grade class from the weight of cans collected by the tenth-grade class.

22 pounds 1 ounce − 18 pounds 14 ounces

Since 14 ounces is greater than 1 ounce, convert 22 pounds 1 ounce to 21 pounds 17 ounces and subtract.

$$
\begin{array}{r}
21 \text{ pounds } 17 \text{ ounces} \\
-18 \text{ pounds } 14 \text{ ounces} \\
\hline
3 \text{ pounds } 3 \text{ ounces}
\end{array}
$$

To convert 3 pounds 3 ounces to ounces, first convert 3 pounds to ounces by multiplying 3 pounds by 16.

3 pounds × 16 = 48 ounces

Then add 3 ounces:

48 ounces + 3 ounces = 51 ounces

Therefore, the correct answer is (C), 51 oz.

52. To determine the approximate value of $\dfrac{199.17}{401.05}$, round the numerator, 199.17, to 200 and round the denominator, 401.05, to 400. The result is $\dfrac{200}{400} = \dfrac{1}{2} = 0.5$.

Therefore, the correct answer is (B); the approximate value is 0.5.

53. The number of computers in a certain school each year is represented by the number of computer symbols.

According to the graph, the number of computers in the year 2000 is represented by 7 computer symbols.

Since each computer symbol represents 5 computers, there were 7 × 5 = 35 computers in the school in 2000.

In 1998 there were 4 symbols, which represents 4 × 5 = 20 computers.

To determine how many more computers were in the school in 2000 than in 1998, subtract the number in 1998 from the number in 2000: 35 − 20 = 15.

Therefore, the correct answer is (B), 15 computers.

54. If $x = 20$ is the solution to $5x = 100$, then when 20 is substituted for x, the left side of the equation should equal the right side.

Given $5x = 100$, to determine the value of the left side of the equation, multiply 5 and 20.

Since 5(20) = 100, the solution is correct.

Therefore, the correct answer is (A). The correct procedure to check the solution is to "Replace the x in the equation with 20, multiply by 5, and check to see if the left and right sides of the equation are equal."

55. To determine which point is NOT inside the square, plot the four points given and label them *A*, *B*, *C*, and *D*, respectively. For example, to plot (5,2) start at the origin and move 5 units to the right and 2 units up.

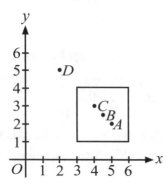

As can be seen on the graph above, the correct answer is (D); (2, 5) is NOT inside the square.

56. Add the fraction of the number of students in Mrs. Brown's class that went to art class, $\frac{2}{5}$, to the number that went to music class, $\frac{1}{3}$:

$$\frac{2}{5} + \frac{1}{3}$$

In order to add two fractions, the fractions must have a common denominator. Since the denominators are 5 and 3, the least common denominator is 15. Convert the fractions so that each has a 15 in the denominator.

$$\frac{2}{5} = \frac{2 \times 3}{5 \times 3} = \frac{6}{15}$$

$$\frac{1}{3} = \frac{1 \times 5}{3 \times 5} = \frac{5}{15}$$

Then add the fractions:

$$\frac{6}{15} + \frac{5}{15} = \frac{11}{15}$$

Therefore, the correct answer is (B), $\frac{11}{15}$.

57. To determine the 5% bonus, convert 5% to a decimal by dividing 5 by 100:

$$\frac{5}{100} = 0.05$$

Then multiply 0.05 by the student's project score of 80:

$$0.05 \times 80$$

To determine the score, including the bonus, add the bonus to the project score of 80.

$$80 + 0.05 \times 80$$

Therefore, the correct answer is (A), $80 + 0.05 \times 80$.

58. Compare the fractions $\frac{1}{4}, \frac{3}{10}$, and $\frac{1}{8}$ by converting all three fractions to fractions with a common denominator.

$$\frac{1}{4} = \frac{10}{40}$$

$$\frac{3}{10} = \frac{12}{40}$$

$$\frac{1}{8} = \frac{5}{40}$$

Then order the fractions by comparing the values of the numerators:

$$5 < 10 < 12.$$

Therefore, the correct answer is (B); the order from least to greatest is $\frac{1}{8}, \frac{1}{4}, \frac{3}{10}$.

59. According to the order of operations, multiplication occurs before addition and subtraction.

Therefore, the correct answer is (D); the first operation in the problem $5 - 3 + 2 + 2 \times 4 =$ is 2×4.

60. To determine Susan's average for the two test scores, divide the total of her two test scores by the number of tests.

Total of two test scores ÷ number of tests = average test score

Since her test scores were 84 and 88, and there were two tests,

$$(84 + 88) \div 2 = 86$$

Therefore, the correct answer is (C); Susan's average of the two tests scores was 86.

WRITING

61. The error in the sentence occurs at (B). The use of the word "several" indicates that the documentary is examining multiple broadcasts, not a single broadcast. Therefore, the word should be plural: "broadcasts."

62. The error in the sentence occurs at (D). The word "than," not the word "then," should be used when introducing the second element in a comparison. Here, the sentence is comparing the potential amount of the profits yielded by strawberries to the potential amount of profits yielded by other crops. Thus, the correct wording here is "can yield more profits per acre **than** almost any other crop."

63. The error in the sentence occurs at (B). The phrase "from Amelia Earhart to contemporary pilot Doris Lockness" is being used to give additional information about the "women pilots." The phrase should be surrounded by commas (grammar books sometimes refer to these phrases as modifying phrases). The sentence does correctly present a comma before this phrase (after "pilots"), but it should also present a comma after the phrase (after "Lockness"). Instead, it presents a semicolon. For this reason, the semicolon that appears at (B) is incorrect.

64. The error in the sentence occurs at (D). The "borders" mentioned in the sentence belong to the "cities and towns" mentioned at the beginning of the sentence. Because "cities" and "towns" are both plural nouns, the possessive adjective used to refer to them should also be plural: "**their** borders."

65. The error in the sentence occurs at (B). The word "frequent" is intended to serve as an adverb modifying the verb "breeds." Adverbs are used to add information about verbs, and they must be placed in what is called "the adverbial form." The adverbial form of "frequent" is "frequently," so the error occurs at (B).

66. The error in the sentence occurs at (C). The sentence is discussing the use of the name Jack in the past—that is, "in the mid-nineteenth century." Thus, the verbs in the sentence should all be in the past tense: "became," "remained," and "declined." Thus, "remains" in answer choice (C) is incorrect because it is in the present tense.

67. The error in the sentence occurs at (D). The subject of the verb "has" is "flavonoids"; because "flavonoids" is a plural noun, the verb should also be plural: "have." Thus, the singular verb "has" in option (D) is incorrect here.

68. The error in the sentence occurs at (D). The sentence indicates that the "active volcanoes" belong to Costa Rica, meaning that the volcanoes are found in that country. To express this "belonging" relationship, the possessive form of the word "country" must be used. The possessive form of "country" is formed by adding an apostrophe followed by an "s": "country's." (D) incorrectly presents "countries," the plural form of "country," instead of the possessive.

69. The correct answer is (A). The main verb in the sentence is "grow"; the subject of that verb is "palms." The other nouns in the sentence ("streams," "mountainsides," "swamps," and "highlands") identify the places where the palms grow, but none of them is the subject of the sentence.

70. The correct answer is (A). The subject of the sentence is "bicyclists," and the simple predicate—the verb that tells what the bicyclists do—is "used." The objects of the verb "used" are "goggles" and "other specialized sports clothing." The rest of the sentence describes the time period during which the bicyclists used the goggles and clothing.

71. The correct answer is (A). The main verb of the sentence is "is thriving"; the subject of that verb is "vision." The adjectives and nouns that follow "vision" ("innovative Italian educator Maria Montessori") and the noun "schools" are used to add information about the "vision" being discussed, but none of them serves as the subject of the sentence.

72. The correct answer is (C). An adverb is a word that modifies a verb, an adjective, or another adverb. Here, "routinely" modifies the verb "condemned," indicating that the critics' condemnation of Wyeth's work occurred on a regular basis.

73. The correct answer is (A). A noun is a word that names a person, place, or thing. Here, "threats" is the name of a thing; it also serves as the subject of the sentence. The sentence goes on to identify the three threats to the survival of the sage grouse.

74. The correct answer is (D). A preposition is a word that is often used to indicate the relationship between a noun or pronoun and another noun or pronoun in the sentence. A preposition usually precedes one of the nouns or pronouns that it is connecting in this way. Here, "in" precedes the noun "structures" and is used to indicate that the "unprotected steel" is within the bounds of, or "in," those "structures."

75. The correct answer is (D). The correct spelling is "village."

76. The correct answer is (A). The correct spelling is "reasonable."

77. The correct answer is (D). The correct spelling is "practical."

78. The correct answer is (C). The correct spelling is "dilemma."

79. The correct answer is (B). Encyclopedia entries routinely list basic information about well-known artists, such as the date and place of their birth. (A) and (C) are not correct because neither source focuses specifically on Yo-Yo Ma. (D) is not correct because the review article concentrates on a particular work of Yo-Yo Ma's and is unlikely to provide facts about his birth.

80. The correct answer is (C). In sentences 1 through 5, Pedro explains why he thinks it is good to have lots of friends. At sentence 6, Pedro begins discussing a new idea: he shifts to discussing the benefits of having just one good friend.

81. The correct answer is (A). Pedro's point in his first sentence is that it's best to have lots of friends. (A) provides another reason why this is true: having a lot of friends provides a network for learning news. (B) does not reinforce Pedro's point because it gives a reason why it's *not* a good idea to have a lot of friends (it can take too much time to try to get them all to like each other). (C) is incorrect because it deals with a completely different topic. (D) does not support Pedro's point because, like B, it gives a reason why it's *not* a good idea to have a lot of friends (it is tiring to keep in touch with them).

82. The correct answer is (C). "Detective fiction" is a subcategory that belongs under the general heading of "Mystery Books."

83. The correct answer is (D). Heading II.A ("Funny Stories") and Heading II.B ("Joke Books") are both specific types of the general category "Humorous Books." (A) is not broad enough to cover all the subheadings under heading II; for example, "Collections of jokes" may be "amusing," but they do not necessarily involve "Amusing Characters."

84. The correct answer is (B). The title and outline of Denise's essay suggest that its purpose is to **inform** the reader about books that people her age like to read, and (B) announces this purpose, using straightforward, unemotional language. (D) begins with the same focus, but it ends with strong language that is intended to comment unfavorably on her fellow students' reading matter. Nothing in the title or outline suggests that Denise intends to criticize anyone or anything, and for this reason (A), with its sarcastic reference

to the library staff and the books, is also inappropriate. The same can be said about (C), which criticizes people who watch too much television.

85. The correct answer is (C). Alexander's paragraph is concerned with discussing how to buy good apples. (A), (B), and (D) do not specifically address the topic of how to select a good apple.

86. The correct answer is (B). According to Alexander, there are three things to look out for when buying an apple: soft spots, dents, and insect damage. (B) provides the most concise and clear list of those three things. (A) is not correct because it is a run-on sentence. (C) and (D) are incorrect because neither one concisely lists the three things to look out for.

87. The correct answer is (B). The word "because" is used to indicate that a reason will be provided for the recommendation provided in the first part of the sentence: it is not good to choose cheap apples, **because** a low price may mean that the apples are getting old.

88. The correct answer is (D), which refers to sentence IV. Sentence IV suggests that the essay will be about what a movie and a television show have in common, and that means that the essay will present a comparison of the ways the two things are alike. Sentence I compares the skateboard to two very different things, but it does so in order to better describe how the skateboard is designed, not to spend equal time exploring the skateboard and the things it is compared to. Neither sentence II nor sentence III indicate that a comparison is being

introduced. Sentence II is most likely the beginning of a persuasive essay, since it states what the school "must" do. Sentence III is most likely the beginning of an instructional (how-to) essay, since it suggests that it will discuss how to make a sock puppet.

89. The correct answer is (B). Sentence II takes a position about what the school must do, indicating that the essay will try to persuade readers that the position is valid. None of the other sentences indicate that author's intention is to persuade readers to adopt a particular viewpoint or understand a particular position. As noted above, sentence I suggests a focus on description; sentence III suggests a focus on instructing the reader as to how to perform an activity (making a sock puppet); and sentence IV suggests a focus on comparing two things.

90. The correct answer is (D). For forming the plural of nouns that end in a -y that is preceded by a consonant, the rule is to change the -y to -i and then add -es. Examples: flies, dictionaries, cities, pennies, puppies, stories.

Chapter 9

Are You Ready? Last-Minute Suggestions

▶ ▶ ▶ ▶ ▶ ▶ ▶ ▶ ▶ ▶ ▶ ▶

Checklist

Complete this checklist to determine if you're ready to take your test.

❑ Do you have your appointment for the computer-based test or your admission ticket for the paper-and-pencil test?

❑ Do you know the topics that will be covered in each section of the test?

❑ Have you reviewed any textbooks, study notes, and course readings that relate to the topics covered?

❑ Do you know how long the test will take and the number of questions it contains? Have you considered how you will pace your work?

❑ Are you familiar with the test directions and the types of questions for your test?

❑ If you are taking the test on computer, have you taken the online tutorial?

❑ Are you familiar with the recommended test-taking strategies and tips?

❑ Have you practiced by working through the practice test questions at a pace similar to that of an actual test?

❑ If you are repeating the *ParaPro Assessment,* have you analyzed your previous score report to determine areas where additional study and test preparation could be useful?

Appendix A
Study Plan Sheet

Study Plan Sheet

See Chapter 1 for suggestions on using this Study Plan Sheet.

STUDY PLAN						
Content covered on test	How well do I know the content?	What material do I have for studying this content?	What material do I need for studying this content?	Where could I find the materials I need?	Dates planned for study of content	Dates completed

Appendix B
For More Information

Educational Testing Service offers additional information to assist you in preparing for the *ParaPro Assessment*. The *Test at a Glance* booklet and the *ParaPro Registration Bulletin* are both available without charge. You can obtain more information from our website: **www.ets.org/parapro.**

General Inquiries

Phone: 609-771-7395 (Monday-Friday, 8:00 A.M. to 8:00 P.M., Eastern time)
Fax: 609-771-7906

Extended Time

If you have a learning disability or if English is not your primary language, you can apply to be given more time to take your test. The *ParaPro Registration Bulletin* tells you how you can qualify for extended time.

Disability Services

Phone: 609-771-7780
Fax: 609-771-7906
TTY (for deaf or hard-of-hearing callers): 609-771-7714

Mailing Address

Teaching and Learning Division
Educational Testing Service
P.O. Box 6051
Princeton, NJ 08541-6051

Overnight Delivery Address

Teaching and Learning Division
Educational Testing Service
Distribution Center
225 Phillips Blvd.
P.O. Box 77435
Ewing, NJ 08628-7435

PLATO® ParaPro Preparation Package

ETS is collaborating with PLATO Learning, Inc. to provide a web-based instructional package to assist paraprofessional personnel in school districts across the country to prepare for the ETS *ParaPro Assessment*. For more information about this product, which is scheduled for release in 2003, contact PLATO Learning at (800) 44PLATO (447-5286), via email at marketing@plato.com, or online at www.plato.com.

Appendix C
Complete List of Topics Covered

▶ ▶ ▶ ▶ ▶ ▶ ▶ ▶ ▶ ▶ ▶ ▶

As you study for the *ParaPro Assessment*, you may find it helpful to have the topics covered in each section of the test listed in one place. This appendix contains representative descriptions of the topics covered in all three categories (reading, math, and writing) of the *ParaPro Assessment*. It does not introduce any new information; all of the topics listed below are also discussed in chapters 4, 5, and 6.

I. Reading Skills and Knowledge

Reading Skills and Knowledge questions measure the examinee's ability to understand, interpret, and analyze a wide range of text. Questions are based on reading passages—as well as tables, diagrams, charts, and graphs—drawn from a variety of subject areas and real-life situations. The questions assess the examinee's ability to

- identify the main idea or primary purpose

- identify supporting ideas

- identify how a reading selection is organized

- determine the meanings of words or phrases in context

- draw inferences or implications from directly stated content

- determine whether information is presented as fact or opinion

- interpret information from tables, diagrams, charts, and graphs

II. Application of Reading Skills and Knowledge to Classroom Instruction

Reading Application questions are typically based on classroom scenarios in which students are involved in reading-related tasks, such as reading assigned passages or working on vocabulary development. Some questions concern *foundations of reading*: the knowledge and skills students need when they are learning the basic features of words and written text. These questions assess the examinee's ability to help students

- sound out words (e.g., recognize long and short vowels, consonant sounds, rhymes)

- break down words into parts (e.g., recognize syllables, root words, prefixes, suffixes)

- decode words or phrases using context clues

- distinguish between synonyms, antonyms, and homonyms

- alphabetize words

Other questions are concerned with *tools of the reading process*: common strategies used in classrooms before, during, and after reading to aid students' reading skills. These questions assess the examinee's ability to

- help students use prereading strategies, such as skimming or making predictions

- ask questions about a reading selection to help students understand the selection

- make accurate observations about students' ability to understand and interpret text

- help students use a dictionary

- interpret written directions

III. Mathematics Skills and Knowledge

The Math Skills and Knowledge questions assess the examinee's knowledge of mathematical concepts and ability to apply them to abstract and real-life situations. The test questions do not require knowledge of advanced-level mathematics vocabulary. Examinees may not use calculators.

Three categories of math skills are tested:

- Number Sense and Basic Algebra

  - Peform basic addition, subtraction, multiplication, and division of whole numbers, fractions, decimals

  - Recognize multiplication as repeated addition and division as repeated subtraction

  - Recognize and interpret mathematical symbols such as $+, <, >, \leq, \geq$

  - Understand the definitions of basic terms such as sum, difference, product, quotient, numerator, denominator

  - Recognize the position of numbers in relation to each other (e.g., $\frac{1}{3}$ is between $\frac{1}{4}$ and $\frac{1}{2}$)

  - Recognize equivalent forms of a number (e.g., $\frac{1}{2} = \frac{2}{4}; \frac{1}{10} = 0.1 = 10\%$)

  - Demonstrate knowledge of place value for whole numbers and decimal numbers

  - Compute percentages

- Demonstrate knowledge of basic concepts of exponents (e.g., $2^2 = 4$, $2^4 = 2 \times 2 \times 2 \times 2 = 16$)

- Demonstrate knowledge of "order of operations" (parentheses, exponents, multiplication, division, addition, subtraction)

- Use mental math to solve problems by estimation

- Solve word problems

- Solve one-step single-variable linear equations (e.g., find x if $x + 4 = 2$)

- Identify what comes next in a sequence of numbers

- Geometry and Measurement

  - Represent time and money in more than one way (e.g., 30 minutes $= \dfrac{1}{2}$ hour; 10:15 = quarter after 10, \$0.50 = 50 cents = half dollar)

  - Convert between units or measures in the same system (e.g., inches to feet; centimeters to meters)

  - Identify basic geometrical shapes (e.g., isosceles triangle, right triangle, polygon)

  - Perform computations related to area, volume, and perimeter for basic shapes

  - Graph data on an xy-coordinate plane

- Data Analysis

  - Interpret information from tables, charts, and graphs

  - Given a table, chart, or graph with time-related data, interpret trends over time

  - Create basic tables, charts, and graphs

  - Compute the mean, median, and mode

IV. Application of Mathematics Skills and Knowledge to Classroom Instruction

The Math Application questions assess the examinee's ability to apply the three categories of math skills listed in Section III (Math Skills and Knowledge) in a classroom setting or in support of classroom instruction. The questions focus on testing mathematical competencies needed to assist the teacher with instruction. The test questions do not require knowledge of advanced-level mathematics vocabulary. Examinees may not use calculators.

V. Writing Skills and Knowledge

Writing Skills and Knowledge questions assess the examinee's ability to identify

- basic grammatical errors in standard written English

- errors in word usage (e.g., their/they're/there, then/than)

- errors in punctuation

- parts of a sentence (e.g., subject and verb/predicate)

- parts of speech (nouns, verbs, pronouns, adjectives, adverbs, and prepositions)

- errors in spelling

VI. Application of Writing Skills and Knowledge to Classroom Instruction

Writing Application questions are typically based on classroom scenarios in which students are planning, composing, revising, or editing documents written for a variety of purposes. Some questions are concerned with aspects of the *writing process*, the full range of activities used when composing written documents. These questions assess the examinee's ability to help students

- use prewriting to generate and organize ideas (including freewriting and using outlines)

- identify and use appropriate reference materials

- draft and revise (including composing or refining a thesis statement, writing focused and organized paragraphs, and writing a conclusion)

- edit written documents for clarity, grammar, sentence integrity (run-ons and sentence fragments), word usage, punctuation, and spelling

Some questions are concerned with *writing applications*, the application of writing for different purposes. These questions assess the examinee's ability to help students

- write for different purposes and audiences

- recognize and write in different modes and forms (e.g., descriptive essays, persuasive essays, narratives, letters)

Please take a moment to complete this review of the *ParaPro Assessment Study Guide*. We appreciate your feedback.

1. Overall, how helpful did you find this study guide?

Very helpful	Somewhat helpful	Neutral	Somewhat unhelpful	Very unhelpful
☐	☐	☐	☐	☐

2. Please rank the different chapters of the study guide in order of helpfulness. Write a **1** next to the most helpful chapter, a **2** next to the second most helpful chapter, and so on.

    _____ Ch. 1: Introduction to the *ParaPro Assessment* and Suggestions for Using this Study Guide

    _____ Ch. 2: Practical Matters: Signing Up for the Test and Tips for the Computer Version

    _____ Ch. 3: Do Tests Make You Nervous? Try These Tips

    _____ Ch. 4: Reading Review Course with Sample Questions

    _____ Ch. 5: Math Review Course with Sample Questions

    _____ Ch. 6: Writing Review Course with Sample Questions

    _____ Ch. 7: Complete Practice Test

    _____ Ch. 8: Right Answers and Explanations for the Practice Test

    _____ Ch. 9: Are You Ready? Last Minute Suggestions

3. Are there parts of the study guide that you would recommend for removal in future editions of the guide?

    ☐ No   ☐ Yes

    If yes, which part(s)? _____

4. Are there any additions to the study guide that you would recommend?

    ☐ No   ☐ Yes

    If yes, please describe _____

    _____

    _____

5. Are there any other changes to the study guide that you would recommend?

    ☐ No   ☐ Yes

    If yes, please describe _____

    _____

    _____

6. Would you recommend this study guide to a friend who is preparing for the test?

    ☐ No   ☐ Yes

7. How many months before the test would you recommend that a person should start studying for the test?

    _____ month(s)

For more information about the ETS Teaching and Learning Division, please visit us at
www.teachingandlearning.org

Thank you for taking the time to complete this feedback form. Please remove the page from the study guide, fold along the dotted lines, and seal with tape before mailing.
We look forward to hearing from you!

Learning Tools
Mail Stop 20-D
PJ 510-54

NO POSTAGE
NECESSARY
IF MAILED
IN THE
UNITED STATES

BUSINESS REPLY MAIL
FIRST-CLASS MAIL   PERMIT NO 89   PRINCETON NJ

POSTAGE WILL BE PAID BY ADDRESSEE

THE PRAXIS SERIES
EDUCATIONAL TESTING SERVICE
PO BOX 6058
PRINCETON NJ 08543-5162